DEVON LIBR
Please return this book on or b

GORDON, Peter   930

The study of the curriculum

375

071342109 6 0 930

Book loans may be renewed by phone or post.

The Study of the Curriculum

edited by
Peter Gordon

Batsford Academic and Educational Ltd.

First published 1981
© Peter Gordon 1981

Batsford Academic and Educational Ltd.
4 Fitzhardinge Street, London W1H 0AH

ISBN 0 7134 2109 6 (cased)
     0 7134 2092 8 (limp)

Reproduced from copy supplied
printed and bound in Great Britain
by Billing and Sons Limited
Guildford, London, Oxford, Worcester

Contents

			page
Acknowledgments			6
Introduction		Peter Gordon	7

Part One   Values and the Curriculum
1	Values and Ideologies	Denis Lawton	11
2	Intelligence and Curriculum	Maggie Ing	20
3	Selection of Knowledge	Peter Gordon	33
4	Organization of Knowledge	Denis Lawton	42

Part Two   Historical and Political
5	Stability and Change in the Curriculum	Peter Gordon	49
6	Concepts of Childhood and the Curriculum	Peter Gordon	60
7	Politics the Curriculum	Denis Lawton	74
8	Accountability	Denis Lawton	81
9	Management and Participation in Curriculum Decision-Making	Peter Gordon	93

Part Three   Curriculum Planning
10	Models of Planning	Denis Lawton	105
11	Cognition and Curriculum I: The Primary Years	Maggie Ing	113
12	Cognition and Curriculum II: Adolescence and Beyond	Maggie Ing	121
13	Theories of Instruction	Maggie Ing	130
14	Motivation and Curriculum Planning	Maggie Ing	138
15	Curriculum Evaluation	Denis Lawton	147

Conclusion	Peter Gordon	158
Bibliography		163
Index		172

ACKNOWLEDGMENTS

The authors and publishers are grateful to the following for permission to quote from the works cited:
R. M. Gagné and the Dryden Press, Holt, Rinehart and Winston for *Essentials of Learning for Instruction*, 1974
B. S. Bloom and the McGraw-Hill Book Company for *Human Characteristics and School Learning*, 1976.

We would also like to thank Lynn Cairns, Val Gregory and Joyce Broomhall for their help in preparing the manuscript; and David Gordon for his assistance with bibliographical and other matters.

Introduction
Peter Gordon

The last 20 years has seen a rapidly growing interest in the study of the curriculum for a number of reasons.

Changes in social and political values have led to an increasing questioning of *what* is taught, i.e. the selection of knowledge; to *whom* it is taught, i.e. knowledge for some or knowledge for all, and *how* it is taught, i.e. the techniques used in teaching. Goodlad (1975) noted that up to a few years ago, curriculum studies was regarded in two different ways. There were those who were mainly concerned with the improvement of classroom instruction which could be evaluated by reference to certain criteria; and those primarily concerned with values inherent in any given curriculum, involving, for example, views of childhood, what knowledge is of most worth and so on. Today, a more eclectic approach is required which takes into account the experience of practitioners, the findings of educational researchers and the contributions made by academic disciplines.

Various definitions of the term 'curriculum' have been put forward. Jenkins and Shipman (1976) suggest that 'The central task in the study of curriculum is to go beyond accurate description to explanation and justification. Reflection on current practices and assumptions is necessary if we are to develop a practitioner's theory and better equip the teaching profession for its participation in the challenge of curriculum renewal'. (p.9). This view is echoed in the Department of Education and Science's Report *Aspects of Secondary Education in England* (1979) which states that: 'Teachers need a view of the school curriculum as a whole and the part they are playing in it if they are to coordinate their pupils' learning and provide them with some sense of coherence in their programmes.' (p.42)

Stenhouse (1975) goes further in defining a curriculum as 'an attempt to communicate the essential principles and features of an educational proposal in such a form that it is open to critical scrutiny and capable of effective translation into practice'. (p.4). These principles would be mainly concerned with the selection of content, the development of a

Introduction

teaching strategy and the finding of a means of evaluating teachers' and students' progress. In an era of accountability, the need to be able to justify the choices made is important.

Neither of these definitions makes explicit the commonly held views of the curriculum. Lawton (1978) outlines three sets of assumptions commonly held by teachers: the child-centred view, as displayed in primary school curriculum, the subject-centred view, associated with secondary or grammar schools, and the society-centred view, which would justify a curriculum in terms of the supposed needs of society. In reality, it is virtually impossible, even if it were desirable, to regard curriculum as less than a unity. For instance, the Report by Her Majesty's Inspectors entitled *Primary Education in England*, 1979, considered the range of curriculum offered, criticized neglected aspects, especially history, geography and science, and called for schools in an area to 'plan their curriculum jointly and with due recognition of society's needs and expectations'.

The subject-centred approach too is under question on two counts: first, there is a growing recognition of interdisciplinary studies and new modes of inquiry-based work which overlap subject boundaries, and, second, schools are, in their curriculum planning, under increasing pressure (see for example *A Framework for the School Curriculum*, 1980) to introduce new 'subjects', such as political and economic education. There are also areas for which no recognized teaching base necessarily exists, for example, careers and social and moral education.

A society-centred curriculum presupposes that the 'needs' of society are known or that it is desirable to plan curriculum directly to meet industrial requirements. The provision of state elementary education in the nineteenth century was largely of such an order. Robin Barrow (1979) remarks in an article 'Back to Basics' that: 'What we need, and will probably get, is what we started out to provide in the past: initiation into the skills, competences and values basic to society, basic operating on a continuum between the very bottom and what the individual is capable of.' (p.202)

Obviously it is not enough simply to agree on a working definition of curriculum. It is important, in examining the field, to understand the changing nature of the contributions to curriculum studies, which are reflected in this book.

The values, explanations and beliefs which underline curriculum activity, in other words one's view of human nature, are, we believe, the starting point for any serious study. This is clearly seen in the various notions which prevail on the nature of intelligence. Mental testing, which goes back to the beginning of the present century, was until recently the basis of selection for different types of secondary schools, each providing

Introduction

different curricula. Subsequent doubts were expressed about the reliability of such testing, stemming from research findings on the socio-economic influences on test scores, from a more critical view of testing techniques and from an increased movement away from behaviourist psychology. The coming of a common system of secondary schooling has led to a reappraisal of the situation.

The simplistic and muddled assumptions of behaviourism (underlined by, for example, Hugh Sockett, 1973, pp.38-45) can be seen not only in the reliance on mental testing, but in the behavioural objectives model of curriculum planning and evaluation. At the present time, it is crucially important to be aware of the assumptions and implications of theories which may be translated into policy. Sociologists in the last decade have turned their attention to the study of curriculum and have raised questions on how knowledge is selected and organized, a field formerly left to the philosophers.

The contributions of psychology, philosophy and sociology do not exhaust the list. To appreciate the rise and fall of 'subjects', the changing attitudes towards the curriculum and the reasons for change or the persistence of tradition, an historical perspective is required to illuminate the scene. As the history of the curriculum is as yet one of the younger disciplines in the field, reference is made in the book to a number of sources which may be useful for further reference. There is also a need to understand the political nature of education decision-making; the substantial literature on the politics of the curriculum is evidence of the attention now being devoted to it at all levels, from individual classrooms to the Department of Education and Science.

The last section of the book shifts the focus away from the macro level to the classroom and deals with aspects of planning the curriculum. This must take account of how children learn, the nature of cognitive development and the learning strategies appropriate to different situations. The handbooks of curriculum projects available to schools bear testimony to attempts to incorporate these findings into the teaching methods to be employed. One important aspect of planning a programme is the need to evaluate the outcomes systematically. Curriculum evaluation is a fairly new art, and is a product of dissatisfaction with the more conventional means of assessment. Some of the evaluation instruments are concerned not only with pupil but with teacher effectiveness. Arising out of this, one of the major issues yet to be decided is the uses to which the information gained should be put. See, for example, the present programme of testing being carried out in schools by the Assessment of Performance Unit at the Department of Education and Science.

It seems likely in the next few years in an era of economic contraction

Introduction

that greater attention will be paid to what can and should feasibly be offered in schools. As the *Secondary School Report*, 1979, states: 'It may be time to think again. Particularly, it may be necessary to develop a more explicit rationale of the curriculum as a whole, which may make it easier to see how far it is realized or realizable in particular structures.' (p.261) It is hoped that this book may be of help to those involved in such planning.

PART ONE
VALUES AND THE CURRICULUM

1
Values and Ideologies
Denis Lawton

There is much discussion today about the fact that we live in a pluralistic society: we do not all share the same values and beliefs. This may be seen as a general problem of social cohesion, but there are also specific relations between a pluralistic society and educational practice which should be examined.

Many aspects of educational policy are dependent on values: for example, the fact that we have had since 1944 a policy of 'secondary education for all' reflects our democratic belief that equality of opportunity is important; the fact that history is taught in schools has something to do with the importance of tradition. But we do not all agree on what kinds of tradition are important or valuable. One of the most basic of these disagreements concerns beliefs about human nature.

Julia Evetts, (1973), for example, divides educationists into two groups with contrasting views of education: the 'idealists' and the 'progressives'. Progressives are said to see education in terms of growth, to see teaching as child-centred rather than subject-centred, and to see the curriculum as an interdisciplinary one, based on the needs and interests of the children; progressives also have views on such topics as intelligence and equality which make the advocates of comprehensive schools and non-streaming. On the other hand, 'idealists' are supposed to see education in terms of acquiring knowledge, to see teaching as initiating pupils into traditional culture, and to see the curriculum organized to transmit an understanding of established disciplines; idealists also tend to approve of selection in education and therefore to dislike comprehensive schools and especially such equalizing devices as mixed-ability groups.

I have elsewhere (Lawton, 1975) expressed dissatisfaction with the clustering together of so many different policies under one label, but to some extent these two opposed views do represent two sets of very basic attitudes and beliefs (this may even be related to what Eysenck (1960) has referred to as the 'tough' and the 'tender' in politics). These two views of education may also, to some extent, be related to what has been described

Values and Ideologies

as the two sociologies or two contrasting views of man in society. (Lawton, 1978, pp. 35-6). For some social and educational theorists, human beings (including children) are essentially evil: for this group the major purpose of education is to stamp out greed, cruelty, selfishness and laziness, and to instil more desirable social and intellectual qualities. By contrast other theorists claim that children are essentially good and naturally virtuous, but are corrupted by society: for them the purpose of education is to allow children to develop 'naturally' and to ensure that they are not corrupted by an evil society.

Hobbes, Durkheim and many nineteenth-century teachers belonged to the 'natural evil' group; Rousseau, Froebel and many others assume children's 'innate goodness'. It would be a mistake, however, to think that these opposing belief systems ever exist in a pure state. Such attitudes and values tend to be much influenced by other social and cultural factors: part of the purpose of this section will be to examine a number of these views in their historical contexts.

Natural Evil

If children are naturally evil then there are many educational implications: freedom will be regarded with disfavour, and the idea of a child-centred curriculum is ludicrous. The purpose of education will be to mould the child into accepted, civilized standards of behaviour. Traditional disciplines and the 'cultural heritage' will be favoured — an extreme version of the doctrine might be 'It doesn't matter what you teach them as long as they dislike it'.

Thomas Hobbes (1588-1679) is often quoted as an early English exponent of the view of man as selfish and therefore needing the control of authority in order to prevent anarchy and chaos. Hobbes was, of course, more concerned with political stability than education, but his general view was that individual selfishness could only be controlled by each individual learning to recognize the need to be protected from others' selfishness, and in return for this protection he would give obedience to a sovereign power. Hobbes' 'egoistic psychology' is clearly relevant, however, to educational practice: children must be disciplined for wickedness and trained to obey authority. Without such discipline civilization would soon disappear. Hobbes has often been criticized for advocating autocratic rule (Rousseau, for example, complained that the social tranquillity achieved by Hobbes' solution would resemble the peace and quiet of a dungeon), but his political concern must be seen against the seventeenth-century background of revolution and social upheaval. At that time he had no difficulty in finding evidence to support his view that man is essentially selfish and could only be improved by society.

Values and Ideologies

Emile Durkheim (1858-1917), a professor ot sociology and education in France, was also concerned with the problem of order in society. Durkheim was worried by the prospect of so much social change that no one would know what the values were (the problem of *anomie*). He felt that one of the functions of education was to induct the young into accepted norms and values (*conscience collective*). Without such a process of socialization human beings would become selfish individuals rather than members of society.

Most nineteenth-century educational practice simply reflected the view of the child as being in need of discipline, correction and civilizing, although there were many varieties of both theory and practice. Thomas Arnold, who was headmaster at Rugby from 1828-42, felt that an essential part of a schoolmaster's work was to repel evil which was partly inherited and partly acquired.

Original sin was inherited from parents; the actual amount of 'sinfulness' varied in individuals, and in some boys would be so great that they would be not only beyond redemption themselves, but would be a harmful influence on others. Expulsion would be the only possible solution in such cases.

The following extract from Arnold's sermons (quoted in Bamford, 1970, pp.86-91) illustrates the link between a view of human nature and an educational programme:

> The six evils in school — profligacy, systematic falsehood, cruelty and bullying, active disobedience, idleness, the bond of evil.
> The actual evil which may exist in a school consists, I suppose, first of all in direct sensual wickedness, such as drunkenness and other things forbidden together with drunkenness in the Scriptures. It would consist secondly in the systematic practice of falsehood — where lies were told constantly by the great majority, and tolerated by all. Thirdly, it would consist in systematic cruelty, or if cruelty be too strong a word, in the systematic annoyance of the weak and simple, so that a boy's life would be miserable unless he learnt some portion of the coarseness and spirit of persecution which he saw all around him.
> Fourthly, it would consist in a spirit of active disobedience — when all authority was hated, and there was a general pleasure in breaking rules simply because they were rules. Fifthly, it would include a general idleness, when everyone did as little as he possibly could, and the whole tone of the school went to cry down any attempt on the part of any one boy or more, to shew anything like diligence or a wish to improve himself. Sixthly, there would be a prevailing spirit of combination in evil and of championship; by which a boy would regard himself as more bound to his companions in ties of wickedness, than to

Values and Ideologies

God or his neighbour in any ties of good—so that he would labour to conceal from his parents and from all who might check it, the evil state of things around him; considering it far better that evil should exist, than that his companions doing evil should be punished.

Let these six things exist together, and the profanation of the temple is complete, it has become a den of thieves.

Then whoever passes through such a school may undoubtedly, by God's grace, be afterwards a good man, but so far as his school years have any effect on his after-life, he must be utterly ruined.

A somewhat different view is that of Edward Thring, headmaster of Uppingham, 1853-87. Thring's solution to the problem of natural wickedness was to make the school a *machine* for overcoming evil!

> Machinery, machinery, machinery, should be the motto of every good school. As little as possible ought to be left to personal merit in the teacher or chance; as much as possible ought to rest on the system and appliances on every side checking vice and fostering good, quietly and unostentatiously, under the commonest guidance and in the most average circumstances. For example, the whole school with few exceptions, is engaged with their masters from seven to nine at night every evening. To the schoolboy eye and casual observer it is a matter of teaching and intellectual guidance, and it is this. But to me it is also that during the two most dangerous hours of the twenty-four every one is under the eye of a master...Trust should be unlimited in action, suspicion unlimited in arrangement, and then there will be no need for it afterwards.
>
> When boys are thrown together under circumstances which no man could be safely trusted in, what is the good of whining over breaches of trust. Let the government be protective, liberal, and individually felt. Then you have a right to expect individual honour, but not otherwise. A certain percentage of crime *must* result from inadequate machinery and neglect.
>
> E. THRING, *Life, Diary and Letters of Edward Thring*, 1898, Volume 1, pp.91-2.

This view of human nature is by no means irrelevant in the study of education today. In recent years the *Black Papers* have returned to the theme of evil:

> It seems indisputable, though alarming, that education, which ought to be particularly concerned with transmitting the heritage of reason

on which civilization is founded has turned its back on reason to a disturbing extent.

A bankrupt and dangerous romanticism is at work, with its roots in the early nineteenth century or even before 'The road of excess leads to the palace of wisdom' (Blake); 'I am certain of nothing but the holiness of the Heart's affections and the truths of Imagination' (Keats); 'Let Nature be your teacher' (Wordsworth). The essential notion is that men are born free and holy, but are crushed by false pressures from the social world. False laws and taboos, inequalities of class, privilege, wealth, colour and creed, are held responsible; the indictment is that all laws imposed on the self from outside contribute to 'man's inhumanity to man'...Today, it has become almost a dogma with many educationists and the unchallenged assumption behind 'self-expression', 'self- fulfilment' as inalienable goods-in-themselves...The essential point, no doubt, is that the traditional ideal of character building has receded too far. Plato, Aristotle, Milton, Locke, Mill, Newman, Arnold—almost every educational theorist of note before our present century—took its prime importance for granted. It is the foundation of much that was great in public and grammar schools. Apollo demands his dues as much as Dionysus. The sleep of reason brings forth monsters.

A. E. DYSON, (1969).

Innate Goodness
Those who believe that children are 'good' but corruptible will stress freedom in education, discovery methods and creativity, and may suggest that it is the teacher's job to 'teach children not subjects'.

The most famous theorist in this tradition was possibly Jean Jacques Rousseau (1712-78) who has in many respects dominated 'progressive' education ever since:

> Let us lay down as an incontrovertible rule that the first impulses of nature are always right; there is no original sin in the human heart...

J. J. ROUSSEAU, *Emile*, 1911 edn.

Children were also seen not simply as miniature adults but as individuals passing through stages which were important in their own right, not merely as a preparation for adult life.

> Nature would have them children before they are men. If we try to invert this order we shall produce a forced fruit immature and flavourless, fruit which will be rotten before it is ripe; we shall have young doctors and old children. Childhood has its own way of

Values and Ideologies

> thinking, seeing and feeling; nothing is more foolish than to try and substitute our ways; and I should no more expect judgment in a ten-year-old child than I should expect him to be five feet high. Indeed, what use would reason be to him at this stage? It is the curb of strength, and the child does not need the curb. *(ibid.)*

On the question of the aims of education, Rousseau was uncompromising: education should not teach children to fit into society but to be free from its shackles:

> The very words 'obey' and 'command' will be excluded from his vocabulary, still more those of 'duty' and 'obligation'; but the words of strength, necessity, weakness and constraint must have a large place in it. *(ibid.)*

In a 'good society' which followed the 'general will' an *adult* would obey, but this would be obedience to his own rational self as expressed in the laws. Adults would thus be both social *and* free in the ideal society. One task of education was to avoid premature, 'irrational' obedience.

Rousseau also had a good deal to say about *how* children should learn, again providing slogans for 'child-centred' educationists ever since.

> A man must know many things which seem useless to a child, but need the child learn, or indeed can he learn, all that the man must know? Try to teach the child what is of use to a child and you will find that it takes all his time. Why urge him to the studies of an age he may never reach, to the neglect of those studies which meet his present needs. But, you ask, 'will it not be too late to learn what he ought to know when the time comes to use it?' I cannot tell; but this I do know, it is impossible to teach it sooner, for our real teachers are experience and emotion, and man will never learn what befits a man except under its own conditions. *(ibid).*

Another well-known example of a theorist dominated by ideas of innate goodness was Friedrich Froebel (1782-1852):

> My teachers are the children themselves with their purity and innocence, their unconsciousness, and their irresistible claims, and I follow them like a faithful, trustful scholar.
>
> in E. LAWRENCE (ed.), *Friedrich Froebel and English Education*, 1952.

Values and Ideologies

Froebel's view of the child was that not only was he pure and innocent but also an expression of divinity; even to suggest that the child was morally neutral was blasphemous. 'Every human being should be viewed and treated as a manifestation of the divine spirit in human form.' *(ibid.)*

He therefore condemned contemporary views which suggested that the child was a lump of clay or wax to be moulded. This optimistic view does not however completely fit in with his views derived from German idealism.

> All the child is ever to be and become, lies, however slightly indicated, in the child, and can be attained only through development from within outward.
>
> in R. R. RUSK, *The Doctrines of the Great Educators*, 1969.

It is interesting that Froebel's theory of opposites did not seem to him to demand a reality of evil as the condition of the reality of good. This inconsistency is pointed out in Nathan Isaacs' chapter in Lawrence, (1952):

> If we turn...to Froebel's actual picture of the child, I think we may say, in the light of our more modern knowledge, that it is far too simple on the one hand and far too idealised on the other. *(op.cit.)*

The purpose of education was, for Froebel, the harmonious development of the child: harmony within the individual, with others and with God. Unlike Rousseau, however, Froebel did not see the development of the individual as being in opposition to the need to adjust to other people in society; Froebel felt that this was esssentially part of the same harmonious development.

Froebel's view of knowledge was an almost mystical belief in unity. Children acquired knowledge of themselves and others by doing things — by activity and structured play. The curriculum was therefore much more a question of methods of developing awareness by means of specific activities. The child is not like a lump of wax to be moulded into the teacher's categorization of knowledge, but is more like a plant which must be allowed space and opportunity to grow as in a well-planned garden. Clearly no detailed curriculum could be planned for this growth — only general principles:

1. Self-activity
2. Connectedness and unbroken continuity
3. Creativeness
4. Physical activity

Values and Ideologies

5. Happy and harmonious surroundings

In many respects Froebel's influence on educational practice was beneficial despite the theoretical flaws, but in terms of curriculum his influence has been to confuse, and the metaphor of the kindergarten has been used to excuse all kinds of sloppy practice:

> Therefore the child should, from the very time of his birth, be viewed in accordance with his nature, treated correctly, and given the free, all-sided use of his powers. By no means should the use of certain powers and members be enhanced at the expense of others, and these hindered in their development; the child should neither be partly chained, fettered, nor swathed; nor, later on, spoiled by too much assistance. The child should learn early how to find in himself the centre and fulcrum of all his powers and members, to seek his support in this, and, resting therein, to move freely and be active, to grasp and hold with his own hands, to stand and walk on his own feet, to find and observe with his own eyes, to use his members symmetrically and equally. At an early period the child should learn, apply and practise the most difficult of all arts; to hold fast the centre and fulcrum of his life in spite of all digressions, disturbances and hindrances.

F. FROEBEL, *The Education of Man*, 1826.

By 1905 a modified version of the child-centred doctrine was 'officially' accepted, and it is probably still the dominant view among HMI and College of Education lecturers:

> The teacher must know the children and must sympathise with them, for it is of the essence of teaching that the mind of the teacher should touch the mind of the pupil. He will seek at each stage to adjust his mind to theirs, to draw upon their experience as a supplement to his own, and so take them as it were into partnership for the acquisition of knowledge. Every fact on which he concentrates the attention of the children should be exhibited not in isolation but in relation to the past experience of the child; each lesson must be a renewal and an increase of that connected store of experience which becomes knowledge. Finally, all the efforts of the teacher must be pervaded by a desire to impress upon the scholars, especially when they reach the highest class, the dignity of knowledge, the duty of each pupil to use his powers to the best advantage, and the truth that life is a serious as well as a pleasant thing. The work of the public elementary school is the preparation of the scholars for life; character and the power of acquiring knowledge are valuable alike for the lower and for the higher purposes of life, and though the teachers can influence only a short

Values and Ideologies

period of the lives of the scholars, yet it is the period when human nature is most plastic, when good influence is most fruitful, and when teaching, if well bestowed, is most sure of permanent result.
Handbook of Suggestions, 1905.

By 1967 this doctrine was associated with a psychology of child development (mostly derived from Piaget, but usually distorted in the process) and enshrined in the Plowden Report, the title of which is itself an expression of the child-centred point of view: *Children and their Primary Schools*. This report was enormously influential, despite such criticism as the collection of papers edited by Professor Richard Peters, 1968, which emphasized the sentimental and naïve doctrine of child-centred education contained in it.

The child-centred ideology is particularly strong for teachers of very young children. King (1979) lists naturalism, individualism, and childhood innocence as the dominant features of this ideology which he showed to be extremely common among infant teachers. He also demonstrated, in a fascinating empirical study, how teachers' practice is not always in complete accord with their theory.

FURTHER READING
A number of useful texts have already been referred to in this chapter, especially King (1979). The best general discussion of the whole issue of values, ideology and the curriculum is contained in an Open University text for their Course E203 (Units 3 and 4) *Culture, Ideology and Knowledge*, 1976, prepared by Malcolm Skilbeck and Allan Harris. An interesting account of how attempts have been made to put progressive educational theory into practice is contained in W. A. C. Stewart, *The Educational Innovators*, 1968, Macmillan.

QUESTIONS
1. Two extreme views have been outlined. What are the possible alternative beliefs about human nature (and especially childhood)? What are the problems of these alternatives?

2. Examine one version of either of the extreme views and:
    (i) comment on the logical consistency of the argument;
    (ii) comment on implications for curriculum planning (preferably, choosing an example not already discussed in the text).

3. Discuss the view of 'the child' contained in either:
    (i) *The Plowden Report*, or
    (ii) *The Lord of the Flies*, by William Golding

2
Intelligence and the Curriculum
Maggie Ing

Beliefs about the nature of intelligence are central to curriculum theory and have influenced educational aims and policies from classroom to national level. In the last hundred years, conflicting concepts of intelligence have been put forward and adopted as working models, more in accordance with prevalent social, political and economic climates than with strict rationality. It would be a mistake to polarize current views, but there are still four main areas of controversy. The two most important are the questions of the relative influence of inherited and environmental factors in intellectual performance, and of the possibility of accurate measurement of intellectual power. Related to these are the theoretical models of the structure of abilities — is 'intelligence' best viewed as a general power, or as a cluster of specific abilities, or some combination of both? — and of the development of mind, as in the work of Piaget, giving rise to a more sophisticated idea of the nature and genesis of intelligence.

The implications for many curriculum questions are far-reaching. Are children sufficiently alike in their mental powers to follow a common curriculum? Can we make them so? Can ability be extended in individuals? Is it sensible to aim for all-round competence for all pupils? Despite more than eight decades of empirical and theoretical study, we have not conclusively answered the most basic questions. This is partly because the very framing of the questions reflects the philosophical stance of the questioners; and partly because the history of empirical studies of 'intelligence' has been inextricably woven with unwarranted theoretical assumptions.

Measuring Intelligence
The first attempt to measure intelligence was essentially pragmatic. Binet's concept of mental age, comparing performance of individual children with others on a variety of tasks, was intended simply to identify backward children in Paris schools. He did not extend this technique into a theory of mind.

...let us recall to mind precisely the limits of the problem for which we are seeking a solution. Our aim is, when a child is put before us, to take the measurement of his intellectual powers, in order to establish whether he is normal or if he is retarded. For this purpose we have to study his present condition, and this condition alone. We have to concern ourselves neither with his past nor his future...As for the future, we shall observe the same restraint; we shall not seek in any way to establish or to prepare a prognosis and we leave the question of whether his backwardness is curable or not, capable of improvement or not, entirely unanswered. We shall confine ourselves to gathering together the truth on his present condition.

A. BINET and T. SIMON, *L'Année Psychologique*, Vol. 2, 1905.

Such restraint was not to last for long. Binet's test was individually administered, and undoubtedly a useful diagnostic tool. With the First World War, group tests were developed. In the USA, the 'Army Alpha' test crudely but effectively sorted out the training potential of thousands of recruits, and in the years after the war, testing on a large scale was used for educational purposes. In Britain, Burt produced standardized tests of educational attainment, based on Binet's 'mental age', giving reading ages, spelling ages, arithmetic ages. His *Mental and Scholastic Tests*, first published in 1921, was widely used and went into its fourth edition in 1962. At the same time, new statistical techniques, especially factor analysis, were being developed, and a theory of the structure of human abilities was emerging.

The legitimate use of descriptive data for diagnosis and educational planning was enthusiastically extended, with insufficient caution over the drawbacks of testing, the likely errors even on well-standardized tests, and both teachers and psychologists confused the theoretical concept of 'intelligence' with the results of intelligence tests. Experimental work in the first three decades of this century showed that IQ (the ratio of mental age to chronological age) tended to remain constant at least up to the age of 15 or 16. This finding is consonant with, but does not prove, the theory that intelligence is a constant power, unaffected by environment. Spearman's proposition of a 'general factor' or g, underlying all mental functioning, pervaded the way in which intelligence was regarded. 'The function appears to become fully developed in children by about their ninth year, and possibly even much earlier. From this moment, there normally occurs no further change even into extreme old age.' (C. Spearman, '"General intelligence" objectively determined and measured', in *American Journal of Psychology*, Vol. 15, 1904.)

Intelligence and Curriculum

A convenient doctrine for a society with unequal distribution of educational resources.

Nature and Nurture

The heredity-environment debate has a long history, and it has been revived in several forms in the last 50 years, the most recent being involved with the question of race and intelligence. Galton (1870) firmly stated the importance of heredity:

> There is no escape from the conclusion that Nature prevails enormously over Nurture when the differences of Nurture do not exceed what is commonly to be found among persons of the same rank of society and in the same country.

Research studies, showing that measured intelligence for many children remains constant, within the limits of errors of measurement, and comparison of twins and studies of fostered children make up the bulk of evidence for the importance of inherited factors. Doubt has been cast on the probity of Burt's twin-study, (see Hearnshaw, 1979, Ch.12), which can no longer be accepted as evidence.

It is important to note that those emphasizing the role of inheritance (even Galton) do not deny the influence of the environment, and those emphasizing the importance of environment do not claim that the inherited potential of everyone is the same, but that, given favourable environmental conditions for all, inherited differences could be less dramatic, and less disabling. Hebb, in *The Organization of Behaviour*, 1949, distinguished Intelligence A, 'innate potential, capacity for development' and Intelligence B, 'the functioning of the brain in which development has gone on, determining an average level of performance or comprehension by the partly grown or mature person'. This remains a statement which most psychologists would accept. Differences arise in assessments of how far, and in what ways, intellectual competence is influenced by environmental factors. Theories, inadequately supported, of the importance of early stimulus, or of the centrality of language, have led to large-scale 'compensatory' programmes with disappointing results.

It is not simply that we are faced with complex technical problems extending over the fields of genetics, neurophysiology and cognitive development, but that our notions of 'intelligence' itself are ill-defined. Embedded values have guided not merely interpretations of data, but the very questions seen as sensible or worthy of investigation.

The 'classical' view of intelligence, summed up by Burt as 'innate, general, cognitive ability', and the confidence of educators and psychologists in the use of IQ tests to determine individual levels of this fixed, innate quality, were based on somewhat naïve assumptions. It was perfectly possible to see intelligence tests as an instrument of social justice, selecting without bias the bright children, regardless of social class, for academic secondary education. These comfortable beliefs, progressive in their time, are reflected in the Norwood Report.

> *Tripartite Organization* Even if it were shown that the differences between individuals are so marked as to call for as many curricula as there are individuals, it would be impossible to carry such a principle into practice; and school organization and class instruction must assume that individuals have enough in common as regards capacities and interests to justify certain rough groupings. Such at any rate has been the point of view which has gradually taken shape from the experience accumulated during the development of secondary education in this country and in France and Germany and indeed in most European countries. The evolution of education has in fact thrown up certain groups, each of which can and must be treated in a way appropriate to itself. Whether such groupings are distinct on strictly psychological grounds, whether they represent types of mind, whether the differences are differences in kind or in degrees, these are questions which it is not necessary to pursue. Our point is that rough groupings, whatever may be their ground, have in fact established themselves in general educational experience, and the recognition of such groupings in educational practice has been justified both during the period of education and in the after-careers of the pupils.

The Norwood Report, 1943.

The three types of pupil are sketched. The grammar school pupil 'is interested in learning for its own sake' and 'can take a long view and hold his mind in suspense'. The technical school pupil, 'whose interests and abilities lie markedly in the field of applied science or applied art' needs a vocational education; while the third type who 'deals more easily with concrete things than ideas' and 'is interested only in the moment', requires a different curriculum again. Twenty years later, the Newsom Report (1963), takes a less dogmatic, and more hopeful, view:

> Intellectual talent is not a fixed quantity with which we have to work but a variable that can be modified by social policy and educational approaches. The crude and simple answer was given by Macaulay 139 years ago: 'Genius is subject to the same laws which regulate the production of cotton and molasses. The supply adjusts itself to the demand. The quantity may be diminished by restrictions and

Intelligence and Curriculum

multiplied by bounties.'

A more subtle investigation into what constitutes the 'restrictions' and the 'bounties' in our society is of far more recent growth. The results of such investigation increasingly indicate that the kind of intelligence which is measured by the tests so far applied is largely an acquired characteristic. This is not to deny the existence of a basic genetic endowment; but whereas the endowment, so far, has proved impossible to isolate, other factors can be identified. Particularly significant among them are the influences of social and physical environment; and, since these are susceptible to modification, they may well prove educationally more important.

The problem is not solely a matter of social conditions. There are still large differences in the progress and attainments of children who appear to start with equal advantages, and even brothers and sisters in the same family differ from each other in talents. Factors of health and growth, character and temperament come into it, as well as native wit, which must be reckoned with, even if it cannot as yet be precisely measured. But when we refer to pupils in this report as 'more able' or 'less able' we are conscious that the terms are descriptive rather than diagnostic; they indicate the facts about the pupil's relative performance in school, but not whether that performance could be modified given different educational approaches.

Half Our Future

The critical influences which disturbed the prevailing notion of intelligence from one Report to the other were from two sources; growing scepticism among psychologists of their own earlier claims, and the body of sociological evidence linking social class factors with intellectual and scholastic performance. The first wave of criticism tended to be reformist in character, pointing out errors and weaknesses of previous work, but not challenging basic values. More recently, there have been radical critiques, both libertarian and Marxist, which question the whole framework of the debate.

Reformist Moves in Psychology

Within the discipline of psychology, there were two distinct movements, one to broaden the earlier concept of 'intelligence', the other to improve techniques of measurement.

1. THE BROADENING OF THE CONCEPT

Spearman's original theory was seen as too simple, and Burt (1940) extended the model of general and specific abilities to include a hierarchy of intermediate factors, although he did not attempt to label all the factors involved. This, at least, moves closer to an accurate representation of the complexity of intellectual performance. J. P. Guilford (1956) classified possible kinds of ability in a still more detailed way:

1. *psychological processes or operations*
   cognition
   memory
   divergent production
   convergent production
   evaluation
2. *kinds of material or content*
   figural
   symbolic
   semantic
   behavioural
3. *forms of products of operations on content*
   units
   classes
   relations
   systems
   transformations
   implications

The interplay of these factors gives, theoretically, $5 \times 4 \times 6 = 120$ abilities. Of course, the factors themselves are hypothetical and could quite conceivably be replaced by others, and their numbers increased or reduced. Factor analysis has not established the independent existence of all 120 postulated abilities and certainly intelligence testing has not expanded to include anything like such a variety. What is important for educators is the emphasis on the *multiple* nature of 'intelligence'. We have tended, and perhaps we still do tend, to combine a global notion of intelligence paradoxically with a restricted notion of the activities in which it can be manifested. Such assumptions would lead to a traditional curriculum, with a high value being placed on a small number of hallowed areas of knowledge; moreover, individuals would be expected to perform fairly consistently on tasks which might when analyzed be very different in their demands. A multi-factor model of intelligence points to the possibility of more accurate mapping of individual strengths and weaknesses, and to the necessity of examining closely just *what* knowledge and skills we want our students to learn. It leads to a view of 'intelligence' not as a *possession*, but as a *series of processes* in different modes, adapted to different outcomes. The curriculum, then, should be diverse, and tailored to individual needs.

Intelligence and Curriculum

It is not only models of ability that were broadened, but the *genesis* of abilities was considered in much greater detail. The work of Piaget became more widely known in the English speaking world, concentrating attention on intelligence as growth, rather than as given. 'Environment'—a term so wide as to be of little practical use—was analyzed in terms of aspects of experience which seemed critical to the acquisition of knowledge and mental strategies. J. McV. Hunt (1961) defined intelligence as 'central processes comprising strategies for processing information that develop in the course of the child's interacting with his environment'. His book is perhaps too eclectic to provide a cohesive theory of intelligence, but he does put the whole issue into the wider perspective of cognitive growth and cultural influence. He firmly rejects the sort of simple arithmetical calculation of the predominance of genetic factors previously accepted.

> ...any policies concerning division of effort in the clinic or classroom based on the commonly quoted answer of a 20/80 percentage split between environment and heredity would be quite wrong.

Pertinently, he asks:

> On the side of manipulating children's encounters with the environment from birth on to maximize intellectual growth, who knows what might be done?

A rigorous and recent attempt to formulate a broad but carefully cumulative theory of intelligence is to be found in Skemp (1979). Starting from an essentially biological view of man, he sees intelligence as 'a quality of those higher mental processes by means of which we become able to direct our activities towards goal states favourable to survival'. Intentionality, emotion, 'inner reality' and social co-operation form parts of his comprehensive view. It is unusual to find humanistic psychology, cognitive and learning theories and social psychology woven into a discussion of intelligence. Even if the thesis might seem over-simple to philosophers and politically naïve to sociologists, it connects and makes sense of previous disparate theories of mental life. Whether or not Skemp's theory will provide the basis for future action, it suggests a better pattern for considering intelligence, combining strong central ideas with a multitude of links to established knowledge of human behaviour in a variety of contexts.

2. Improving Techniques Of Measurement

Alice Heim (1954) incisively laid bare the flaws inherent in intelligence

Intelligence and Curriculum

testing. As a student of psychology, I was advised *not* to read her book before the standard works on psychometrics, lest I should become too cynical — advice which naturally led me to read the book immediately, at a sitting, with exactly the predicted effect. She lists five major sources of unreliability in mental testing.

(i) The test itself may be a poor measuring instrument, in the sense that a fairly taut piece of elastic would be a poor instrument for measuring the length of, say, a bookcase. The analogy might even be extended, bearing in mind certain tests, to using a pair of scales, with weights of unknown value, for measuring the temperature of the bath water!

A major problem in test construction is that we *cannot* assume that all questions are 'equal', like inches on a tape measure; nor can we assign reliable differences to 'weighted' questions. Using tests developed for one population on another would also give highly unreliable results.

(ii) The quality being tested may be intrinsically variable, if, indeed, we are justified in postulating such a 'quality' at all.

(iii) Circumstantial effects are known to affect test results. Time of day, the tester's technique, illness of the testee are only a few of the circumstances which can make a difference to scores — and not necessarily the *same* difference to individuals. Several studies (Deutsch *et al*, 1968, Watson, 1972) have demonstrated that black children score better on tests with a black tester.

(iv) Practice and coaching, even on different tests, can raise scores. Vernon (1956) estimated a maximum rise of 12 to 15 points.

(v) 'Observer error', by which Heim means all errors of technique or scoring, including slips made by the testee, can easily creep into tests and be undetected.

These are not the only sources of unreliability, but merely 'those which are inherent in the whole notion of intelligence testing and which cannot be eliminated by improved tests'. Subsequently, Heim has devoted years to the construction of improved tests. Examples can be seen in Heim (1970).

The educational use of such imperfect measures came in for criticism. Pidgeon and Yates (1968) showed that as many children 'over-achieved' as 'under-achieved' in relation to their measured intelligence, which shows the absurdity of using IQ scores to guide teachers to choose an appropriate curriculum. Ought we to rein back 'over-achievers' or somehow deny their educational progress? P. E. Vernon (1957) maintained that, even with the best standardized tests, sampling errors

Intelligence and Curriculum

alone led to the misplacing of 5 per cent of secondary school children. Disillusion had set in, but most psychologists did not completely reject testing.

It seems to me that intelligence tests are bound to be unreliable in some ways, however carefully they are constructed and administered. But they are almost certainly no less reliable than other methods of assessing human capacity nor are they lacking in value as instruments for research and individual diagnosis. (Heim, 1954)

Social Class and Intelligence

It is not possible here to give an adequate account of the mass of evidence produced in the 1950s and 60s that school attainment, measures of intelligence, and consequently educational opportunities, are linked to social class factors, rather than residing in some innate properties of individuals. If intelligence is dynamic, capable of growth and development, it follows that experience, at home, in the community and at school, must crucially affect competence. Moreover, as the Early Leaving Report (1954) and the Robbins Report (1963) pointed out, even those working-class children deemed able to pursue an academic education were less likely to seize their opportunities than middle-class children of no greater, and sometimes less, ability. The general tendency of research was to look for explanations 'in the experiences and attitudes of the working-class family' (Banks 1963). Floud, Halsey and Martin (1957), Fraser (1959), Jackson and Marsden (1962), Wiseman (1964), Douglas (1964) are representative of the research of the time. Briefly summarized, the important variables seemed to be:

1. parental attitudes to education
2. level of education of parents
3. family size
4. maternal care
5. material prosperity – at least where real poverty was involved.

Bernstein's early work on language (1961, 1965), although within a rather different theoretical framework, was certainly interpreted as underlining another critical variable. The problem could then be seen as one of remedying the deficiencies in the child's background; difficult to accomplish of course, but clear-cut in theory.

Thus the Plowden Report (1967):

> The research and surveys cited, and much else to the same effect, suggest that we are far from realizing the potential abilities of our

Intelligence and Curriculum

children. To reveal the influence of parental occupation is a criticism of society; but it is also an opportunity for reform. There must always be a great diversity of parental occupations; but they need not continue to have their present severe discriminatory effect on children's educational prospects. The grosser deprivations arising from poverty can be removed. More parents can be brought to understand what education can do for their children, and how they can work with the schools. The educational disadvantage of being born the child of an unskilled worker is both financial and psychological. Neither handicap is as severe as it was. Both are more severe than they need be. Educational equality cannot be achieved by the schools alone: but the schools can make a major contribution towards ensuring (as Sir Edward Boyle wrote in his foreword to the Newsom Report) 'that all children should have an equal opportunity of acquiring intelligence.' (para.85)

The recommendations (paras. 174-7) set out the ways in which 'positive discrimination' should achieve this happy end.

Culture and Intelligence
Explicit in reformist theory and policy is the notion that intelligence is best developed where the values of home, neighbourhood and school are in harmony; implicit is the notion that one *particular* culture is clearly more desirable. Lawton (1975) discusses in detail the question of culture, which cannot be expanded here. One off-shoot of the increased realization that measures of intelligence may substantially reflect experience rather than potential was the attempt to devise 'culture-free' and 'culture-fair' tests (e.g. P. E. Vernon, 1965, 1966, 1967). Such endeavours could never have more than limited success, as even the perception of non-verbal items must be somewhat influenced by experience, and may well be mediated by language; while attitudes to being tested at all vary between cultures (Warburton 1951). Cross-cultural differences in the rate of development according to Piaget's stages have been found (Greenfield in Bruner, 1966) where the items themselves are more nearly universal than those in most intelligence tests.

It would be too simple to suggest that through the 1950s and 60s the evident mis-match between the intellectual functioning of children and the aims of schools was blamed entirely on the children's deficient culture. Schools, too, came in for censure. Peaker (1967) estimated that 17 per cent of the variation in attainment among English primary school children could be attributed to variables in schools. Douglas (1964) found that schools with a good record of achieving grammar school

Intelligence and Curriculum

places increased their pupils' chances by 20 per cent more than their test scores at 11 would have predicted. Jackson's (1964) study of streaming foreshadowed Rosenthal and Jacobson (1966) in the claim that teachers' expectations influenced pupils' performance. Barnes (1969) found that the language used by teachers in secondary schools often hindered learning. The social organization of schools was seen as inimical to some pupils' development (Hargreaves, 1967, Lacey, 1970).

But each of these shifts of responsibility, from deficient individuals, to deficient families and cultural patterns, to deficient teachers and schools, seems inadequate. Whatever partial truths have been revealed, there is an unpleasant flavour of scapegoat-hunting and a lack of comprehensiveness in them all.

Radical Critiques

At best, the radical critiques of the 1970s provide a much-needed political dimension to the way we conceptualize intelligence and place education within the wider context of the whole socio-economic structure of society. At worst, 'the system' becomes the scapegoat, with sinister hints of conspiracy against the majority of the people.

There is no large, established body of radical psychology theory to which the reader can be referred; the determined isolation of the subject from both philosophy and sociology — partly the result of the dominance of behaviourism for so many decades and itself an example of the ritualization and academic territory-defining underlined by radical theorists — has left it largely conservative and, all too often, conceptually naïve. Much of the criticism of notions of intelligence comes in the form of side-swipes from sociologists (see Esland in Young, 1971). Smith (1977, Ch.5) collects together from the alternative press some lively and pertinent comments on the uses and abuses of testing. One of the most concise applications of radical theory to psychology is Ingleby's paper in Pateman (1972). Reform, he claims, is not enough: 'The cry of "put your house in order" must be resisted if it is going to be taken to mean that the house itself is structurally sound.'

In his view, the structure is far from sound; ideology permeates the supposedly objective, neutral norms of psychology as a human science.

> In the first place, we are led to suppose that the psychologist is the guardian of everything which must be understood in terms of the acting human subject...In practice the psychologist appears to be more anxious to sell out to some other variety of science, and to reduce human realities to some other non-human, reality...

Intelligence and Curriculum

His account of *reification*, the process by which human qualities are reduced to the order of *things*, seems particularly applicable to the notion of intelligence and the uses to which it has been put. The labelling of children on some spuriously objective scale of intelligence demonstrably has eliminated some human possibilities; and, as Ingleby points out, from the effects of such classifications there is little chance of appeal.

His conclusion that 'a genuinely objective science of man must always be aware of its own ideology if it is to take any action against the biases that ideology imposes', shows the need for a much more searching look at our assumptions about intelligence and the values inherent in them. It is hard to question the truth of what we take as certain; it is even harder to know what to do with the resultant uncertainties.

Conclusion

In summary, there are at least three major sources of difficulty in creating a notion of intelligence which does justice to the complex and active nature of human abilities. The first is semantic; the noun 'intelligence' is convenient, but a constant temptation to reify, to see multiple, fluctuating powers as a kind of mental muscle.

The second is our habit of valuing intelligent activity *only* over a comparatively narrow range of symbolic manipulations. This is linked to the knowledge and skills valued in our society. Whether or not we accept that the 'legitimation' of knowledge *always* has an economic basis and is used as a form of social control, we certainly need to consider radically and rationally the values contained in our curricula. (I am not suggesting that this is the duty of teachers alone).

The third problem springs from the first; if we see intelligence as an entity, we are misled into scaling persons according to 'how much' of it they possess. The whole nature/nurture question is pointless. It is not possible to disentangle some pure, genetic factor of brain-efficiency, since the capacity to act intelligently depends in any one instance on a whole range of individual and circumstantial factors.

Finally, irreducible beliefs about the nature of human beings, emphasizing differences or similarities, possibilities or limitations, will inevitably colour our theories of intelligence and their outcome in action.

FURTHER READING

A. W. Heim, *The Appraisal of Intelligence*, 1954, an incisive account of the limits of testing from the point of view of a psychologist who sees some value in the attempt to measure ability.

L. S. Hearnshaw, *Cyril Burt: Psychologist*, 1979. Chs.4 and 12, a sympathetic but fair view of Burt's early formulation of 'intelligence' and the posthumous suspicions and controversies about his evidence.

Intelligence and Curriculum

H. J. Butcher, *Human Intelligence Its Nature and Assessment*, 1968. Chs.7, 8, 10, 11. A sound over-view of the literature up to 1968. Ch.10, 'Social and cultural influences' is a useful summary.

QUESTIONS
1. 'The witch-doctor, the prince-bishop, the baron, the emperor have all proclaimed the power of inborn factors; the reformer, the republican, the radical, the revolutionary have emphasized the equality of man and the potentiality of education, training and a favourable environment. It is, therefore, a social and political question first, and an educational question second.' S. Wiseman, *Education and Environment*, 1964.
How far do you agree?
2. How far do you agree that intelligence tests are an inappropriate basis for allotting pupils to different curricula?

3
Selection of Knowledge
Peter Gordon

No one would today claim that there is such a thing as a 'natural' curriculum. Whatever activity, form of teaching or organization of schooling is adopted, choices have to be made in the way that knowledge is presented. Entwistle (1970) saw the subject curriculum as representing the different ways in which we have learnt to structure and codify knowledge of ourselves and the universe. This will include the physical environment and the civilized arts.

> ...the distinctive academic disciplines are merely attempts to explore, organize, extend and make explicit what we already know, intuitively, about the common experience of daily life, as well as providing the instruments of self-discipline whereby we develop our understanding, our interests and our tastes.
> H. ENTWISTLE, *Child-Centred Education*, 1970, p.101.

One problem which has always faced educationists is the difficulty of translating such aims into classroom practice. Obviously, the labels attached to subjects and the constellation of subjects offered as a curriculum differ from age to age, according to the prevailing philosophy on the nature of schooling and the attitudes towards the recipients of such a curriculum. It is important, then, before we can make any valid judgments on the school subjects considered appropriate at any given time to examine what they represent.

The 'grammar' school curriculum of the Middle Ages is the most obvious and at the same time most often misunderstood example of the danger of generalizing. Such a school is often depicted as having been devoted almost exclusively to the study of Greek and Latin by order of its pious founders. In fact, the curriculum was based on a seven-fold division which, whilst looking to classical authorities for its justification, was fairly liberal in character.

Varied as these grammar schools must have been in their external

Selection of Knowledge

organization throughout the Middle Ages, there was, besides, considerable difference in the importance attached to the relative position of 'grammar' in the curriculum at various periods. The curriculum of earlier education, at its fullest, consisted of the seven liberal arts, i.e. the trivium consisting of grammar, dialectic (or logic) and rhetoric, and the quadrivium, viz. arithmetic, music, geometry and astronomy. These seven arts were regarded as the intellectual equipment with which the theologian, the doctor and the lawyer might start out to solve by disputational processes the problems relating to professional practice. The Medieval Ages were dominated by authority — and in the period of Scholasticism regarded Aristotle as the final court of appeal. The trivium was the elementary equipment necessary for younger pupils. Even in the time of the Commonwealth a contemporary writer speaks of Eton as a 'trivial' school, meaning a school in which grammar, dialectic and rhetoric were originally taught. It is essential to realise that the earlier medieval schools, even if they claim to be grammar schools, did so usually in recognition of the Roman usage; for in ancient Rome the scholars had studied language and literature under the name of grammar. But the later medieval schools, with both the younger and the older pupils, laid their chief stress on the logic and dialectic which prepared the skilled student for metaphysical subtlety. Even the small amount of grammar studied was surrounded by 'glosses', and belonged more to metaphysics than to linguistics.

F. WATSON, *The Old Grammar School*, 1916, pp.5-7.

The Church monopoly of education is reflected in this quotation and changes were slow to come. By the seventeenth century, even though there had been important advances in men's thinking in England, the range of school subjects remained unchanged. Charles Hoole's book *New Discovery of the Old Art of Teaching Schools*, 1660, which gives a detailed picture of contemporary school curriculum, indicates that the Bible, the Psalter and the Primer were used for teaching spelling and reading. Much of the liveliness of earlier times, as in the teaching of Rhetoric for instance, had been reduced to synopses from textbooks.

The source of changes in thinking had arisen from rapid advances during the seventeenth century in the scientific field, where the study of astronomy, anatomy and mathematics had flourished. Followers of Francis Bacon's 'new philosophy', (that is the study of natural phenomena on inductive principles through observation and experiment) especially senior members of universities, met together to form the 'Invisible College'. This ultimately led to the establishment of the Royal Society in 1662. The implications of this new knowledge for the curriculum were made explicit by two notable educationists, Comenius and Hartlib, at this time.

Comenius, a Bohemian who lived well into the seventeenth century, had been attracted by the work of Francis Bacon. Convinced of the need for observation and experiment at first hand as the basis for natural science, he was keen to extend the curriculum in schools and universities to include new discoveries in science.

> He believed that scientific study would induce a new attitude of mind towards knowledge generally and its acquisition. The attainment of knowledge he regarded, with Bacon, as rather a question of method than of individual capacity; and the method of instruction which he pressed upon his contemporaries was one which was to be governed by an understanding of mental process as it exists and develops in immature minds. It was regarded almost as axiomatic by educational reformers of that day, that given the correct method, the possibility of learning was well-nigh infinite; Bacon was responsible for an error which Milton in the tractate *Of Education* very fully exemplified. On that ground, Comenius saw no difficulty in adding to the accepted subjects of school study those modern subjects, such as history, geography and, above all, the vernacular, whose omission had become a reproach. Such were some of the principles of Comenius's *The Great Didactic (Art)*, *setting forth a universal system of teaching everybody everything*, a work written between 1628 and 1632.

J. W. ADAMSON, *A Short History of Education*, 1919, pp.182-3.

Samuel Hartlib, a Prussian-born English educational reformer, was responsible for the publication of Comenius' work in England. One result of the spread of Comenius' ideas was the formulation of a revolutionary scheme by William Petty who was a physician and an economist: that the school curriculum should be based chiefly on the principle of utility.

> Petty would erect schools which all *children*, not boys only, must attend after reaching the age of seven; poor children should be assisted by scholarships. The course of instruction begins with observation of 'all sensible objects and actions, whether they be natural or artificial, which the educators must on all occasions expound unto them', that is, by object lessons, as we should say. After that come reading, writing and shorthand. All are to learn these things as well as drawing, physical exercises, the elements of arithmetic and algebra, and, above all, a handicraft. Music may be learned by those who have a talent for it and foreign languages by those only who will need to use them.

ibid., pp.183-4.

Selection of Knowledge

The coming of the Industrial Revolution raised the question of providing mass education for an industrial nation. As Raymond Williams (1961) pointed out, the first new educational institutions were the industrial schools which gave manual training and elementary instruction, and Sunday Schools, which were to counteract dangerous and possibly revolutionary ideas. At the same time, the desire of the new middle classes for a wider provision of schooling led to an expansion on the lines of the 'public' schools, and with a similar curriculum. The two 'traditions' of English education, that based on classics for the middle and upper classes and that based largely on the three Rs for the rest, were established. Matthew Arnold, one of the leading champions of the middle classes, saw culture, and especially the pursuit of perfection, as a social idea which would ultimately lead to a narrowing of differences between classes.

> The great men of culture are those who have a passion for diffusing, for making prevail, for carrying from one end of society to the other, the best knowledge, the best ideas of their time; who have laboured to divest knowledge of all that was harsh, uncouth, difficult, abstract, professional, exclusive; to humanize it, to make it efficient outside the clique of the cultivated and learned, yet still remaining the *best* knowledge and thought of the time, and a true source, therefore, of sweetness and light.

M. ARNOLD, *Culture and Anarchy*, 1868-9.

In reality, the gulf between the two classes remained large. This can be seen in looking at the array of subjects offered in a typical secondary and elementary school in the last quarter of the nineteenth century. The first is from a report of a boy at Eton in 1893, which shows that two-thirds of the marks awarded for the form examination were in respect of classical subjects.

Papers		Max. Marks
Divinity		100
Translation	Greek / German	140
Translation	Latin	140
Grammar	Latin / Greek / German	100

Selection of Knowledge

Papers	Max. Marks
Latin Prose	100
Verses	100
History and Geography	100
Classical Total	780
Mathematics	200
French	100
Science	120
Maximum Total	1200

In contrast, here is an analysis of the work of a 'top' class at a Northumberland elementary school in 1879.

Curriculum	Number of hours per week
Transcribing	10¼
Reading	9½
Arithmetic	5¾
Scripture and Catechism	2½
	28

Two years after the publication of Darwin's *Origin of Species*, Herbert Spencer's work *Education: Intellectual, Moral and Physical* (1861) appeared. Its particular value to the present discussion lies especially in the first chapter, 'What Knowledge is of Most Worth?'. The choice of subjects which may be taught to a child, stated Spencer, is almost unlimited and nearly all will be of value in adult life. But given the fact that the actual amount that can be learnt is limited, some principles of selection must be formulated. Spencer therefore set out a classification, in order of importance, of the leading kinds of activity which constitute human life. They are, in Spencer's order, those which

1. directly minister to self-preservation;
2. after securing the necessaries of life, indirectly minister to self-preservation;
3. relate to the rearing and discipline of offspring;
4. are involved in the maintenance of proper social and political relations;
5. occupy the leisure part of life.

Spencer appreciated that the five divisions overlapped, but nevertheless

Selection of Knowledge

believed that the ideal of education is to provide complete preparation in all these divisions. As can be seen from the following passage, Spencer concludes that from a utilitarian point of view, science is of far greater value than any other subject.

> In regulating education by this standard, there are some general considerations that should be ever present to us. The worth of any kind of culture, as aiding complete living, may be either necessary or more or less contingent. There is knowledge of intrinsic value; knowledge of quasi-intrinsic value; and knowledge of conventional value. Such facts as that sensations of numbness and tingling commonly precede paralysis, that the resistance of water to a body moving through it varies as the square of the velocity, that chlorine is a disinfectant, — these, and the truths of Science in general, are of intrinsic value: they will bear on human conduct ten thousand years hence as they do now. The extra knowledge of our own language, which is given by an acquaintance with Latin and Greek, may be considered to have a value that is quasi-intrinsic: it must exist for us and for other races whose languages owe much to these sources; but will last only as long as our languages last. While that kind of information which, in our schools, usurps the name History—the mere tissue of names and dates and dead unmeaning events—has a conventional value only: it has not the remotest bearing on any of our actions; and is of use only for the avoidance of those unpleasant criticisms which current opinion passes upon its absence. Of course, as those facts which concern all mankind throughout all time must be held of greater moment than those which concern only a portion of them during a limited era, and of far greater moment than those which concern only a portion of them during the continuance of a fashion; it follows that in a rational estimate, knowledge of intrinsic worth must, other things equal, take precedence of knowledge that is of quasi-intrinsic or conventional worth...
>
> These, then, are the general ideas with which we must set out in discussing a *curriculum:* Life as divided into several kinds of activity of successively decreasing importance; the worth of each order of facts as regulating these several kinds of activity, intrinsically, quasi-intrinsically, and conventionally; and their regulative influences estimated both as knowledge and discipline.

H. SPENCER, *Education: Intellectual, Moral and Physical* (1861) 1889 edition, pp.11-12.

Selection of Knowledge

Spencer's critics have held that he overstates the claims for science; that it is based too much on rationality; that living languages have greater value in later life than Spencer admits; that the universality of these ideas would be difficult to achieve; and that they are theories most suitable to Spencer's own rather than children's minds. Nevertheless, the classification of human activities is an interesting one, taken with the following chapters in the book on intellectual and moral education. Some affinities with Rousseau's ideas are noticeable in Spencer's views, notably that education should lead from the simple to the complex and from the indefinite to the definite.

More recently, attention has shifted from the most desirable selection of subjects in a curriculum to that of organizing a curriculum according to desired objectives. Hirst and Peters (1970), in considering this approach, also discuss the nature of integration of subjects. The traditional curriculum is organized into a number of subjects planned without reference to one another, each with a limited range of objectives. They point out for example, that under English or geography or religious education, several types of understanding might be sought at the same time. It would be better to plan a curriculum composed of different units, some devoted perhaps to a single mode of experience and knowledge, as in mathematics, or where the teacher may be concerned with objectives taken from several different modes, as in geography.

At a more detailed level, Pring (1976) puts forward a case for integration. In the lower secondary school, it is argued, there are three reasons for advocating an integrated curriculum.

> Firstly, the respect for the varied mental activities of the pupils to be educated, secondly, a recognition of the commonsense language and understandings through which the pupils already engage in this mental life and to which the more disciplined modes of enquiry must be related, and thirdly, the need for a more flexible and cooperative teaching framework in which different teacher resources can be brought into contact with so many individual differences.
>
> R. PRING, *Knowledge and Schooling*, 1976, p.120.

One question which arises from this is how can the traditional selection of a culture, as reflected in school subjects, be co-ordinated with children's ways of thinking? Reynolds and Skilbeck (1976) show, for example, that we often fail to remember that certain words, such as education, marriage and work represent or codify experience, an experience which pupils

Selection of Knowledge

lack. The authors look more to the need to impart in the first place the techniques of acquiring knowledge by helping them to empathize, to develop imaginative ideas and to reinterpret some of the basic modes of experience. These, however, are seen as short-term aims. The long-term aim is to look for common denominations in the critical use of symbols underlying science, arts and humanities and in the everyday thought and feeling of people. Both can make use of similar strategies for solving problems and can illustrate the importance of relating symbolic forms to reality and developing shared understanding.

It would be well to remember however that some educationists reject the notion that it is realistic or profitable to refer to or assume a shared culture. According to Bantock (1965) the notion of equality makes for difficulties in establishing a system of education adjusted to the different levels of cultural and mental capacities in the community. Many pupils, because of their background, are unable to take advantage of the literate culture advanced in schools. This, Bantock claims, is because historically and psychologically, they are not prepared for such a diet as it is not consonant with their traditional way of living. The rejection of such a culture by pupils after leaving school, to be replaced by affectively based media-communicated culture, is a witness to this.

To the sociologists of knowledge, Bantock's statement would confirm their view that there is a social basis for different subjects; that teachers determine what is to count as knowledge; and that the definition of knowledge represents 'conscious or unconscious cultural choices which accord with the values and beliefs of dominant groups at a particular time' (M. F. D. Young, *Knowledge and Control*, 1971, p.38). The curriculum offered in schools demonstrates how knowledge is stratified. High status knowledge, as seen in the academic curriculum, is characterized as emphasizing the literary, a concern with the written rather than the spoken word, abstractness of knowledge structured independently of the learners and knowledge at odds with daily life and common experience. Low status, i.e. non-academic curricula, are, by this definition, organized in terms of oral presentation, group activity and assessment and concreteness of knowledge. Thus, this approach pays attention not only to the nature and content of subjects but to their distribution within schools.

This relativist view of knowledge has been valuable in drawing attention to problems of operating a curriculum, although it fails to distinguish between different *kinds* of knowledge, denies the existence of a common body of knowledge and pays little acknowledgement to the necessity of making choices in curriculum planning (Warnock, 1977).

The selection of knowledge is obviously reflected in the ways it can be organized and the following chapter will describe some of them.

Selection of Knowledge

FURTHER READING

For a useful starting point, see K. Harris, *Education and Knowledge*, 1979, Ch. 1. The essays in P. H. Hirst, *Knowledge and the Curriculum*, 1974, should be consulted. A comparatively old but interesting text is S. Nisbet, *Purpose in the Curriculum*, 1957, 8th impression 1974, especially Ch. VII.

QUESTIONS

1. Can we differentiate between skills and subjects?
2. To what extent is it fruitful to regard knowledge, in terms of the school curriculum, as problematical?

4
Organization of Knowledge
Denis Lawton

T. W. Moore (1974) suggests that any educational theory must include assumptions about a) aims; b) the nature of human beings (in particular, children), and c) the nature of knowledge and how to transmit it. In this section we are concentrating on assumptions about knowledge. Not only is an educational theory incomplete unless it includes some kind of theory of knowledge, but it must also be true that it is impossible for a teacher to teach without making assumptions, implicit or explicit, about the nature of knowledge. At a fairly obvious level, it is certainly true that the language which we have been brought up to use encourages us to believe that geography *is* different from physics or anthropology, even if we are not sure exactly where the boundaries lie. Are these differences mere conventions? Or are there good philosophical reasons for sub-dividing knowledge into such categories?

There are no clear-cut, easy answers to those questions. And the difficulties are compounded by the fact that an educated person's view of knowledge is partly a matter of philosophical analysis (epistemology), and partly a question of social tradition: for example, philosophers would agree that mathematics is identifiably different from poetry by a number of well-established criteria such as the concepts and methods used, and what counts as truth or excellence. That is a very clear, probably uncontroversial example. But what about the distinction made in universities and elsewhere between sociology and anthropology, for example? Isn't that kind of distinction simply the result of individual scholars grouping themselves together in certain ways, in various institutions, partly by choice, partly by accident and then wishing to preserve their corporate identities? Do these two subjects overlap so much that they might easily be grouped together (as in fact they are in some universities)? If so, is this a good example of the 'social construction of knowledge'?

One danger to be avoided is to take an 'all or nothing' approach to these questions: if you 'prove' that the distinction between sociology and

Organization of Knowledge

anthropology is less important than the similarities, this neither demonstrates that all barriers are artificial nor that there are no important differences between mathematics and literature. The existence of some subjects or disciplines may be simply a question of tradition, but others may be philosophically justifiable. One of the tasks is to clarify which are which.

It is also important to clarify the relation between the *logic* of the disciplines and the *psychology* of teaching and learning. Sorting out knowledge into disciplines and subjects may help curriculum planners to decide what everyone needs to know, but that decision does not necessarily predetermine *how* learning should be organized at the level of a timetable. If we decide, for example, that all eight year olds ought to learn mathematics, science, language, etc., it does not cut out the possibility of an 'integrated day' approach or any other kind of interdisciplinary organization. Decisions about the structure of knowledge may influence the organization of learning, but we should also always bear in mind psychological factors such as motivation, interests, attention span and so on. We should also remember that the psychological evidence is conflicting: some writers stress the need to make the most of children's own interests; others stress the need for children to get inside the structure of the discipline.

There is a long history of sub-dividing the curriculum according to different kinds of knowledge. You may wish to try to decide the extent to which some of these are logical categories or mere conventions. The medieval curriculum, for example, was made up of the seven liberal arts: grammar, rhetoric and logic (the trivium); and arithmetic, music, geometry and astronomy (the quadrivium). Since then knowledge has expanded, and today different categories are used, so much so that basing a curriculum on these seven categories now seems somewhat curious to us.

In recent years philosophers of education have been concerned to relate the structure of knowledge to curriculum planning in a number of ways — for example, G. W. Ford and L. Pugno in 1964 edited a collection of papers called *The Structure of Knowledge and the Curriculum* (which was influential in the USA). One of the contributors to that volume, J. J. Schwab, traced the origin of this kind of analysis back to Greek philosophy. Aristotle identified three classes of disciplines — the *theoretical* (metaphysics, mathematics, natural science); the *practical* (ethics, politics); and the *productive* (fine and applied arts, engineering).

Schwab was content to remain with only three kinds of discipline but classified them differently: the *investigative* (natural sciences), the *appreciative* (arts), and the *decisive* (social science).

This was too simple for Broudy who, following Tykociner, needs five

Organization of Knowledge

groups of disciplines:

1. *symbolic* (including language, logic and 'the language of art');
2. *systematizing* (the basic sciences with structured conceptual systems);
3. *evolutionary* (history, biography, etc. giving order to the past);
4. *problem-solving* (agriculture, medicine, technology, etc.);
5. *integrative/inspirational* (philosophy, theology, art).

In the UK perhaps the most influential philosopher has been Paul Hirst: 'A liberal education can only be planned if distinctions in forms of knowledge are clearly understood'. Hirst points to a logical demarcation of knowledge in seven non-overlapping sub-divisible 'forms' arising from distinctive kinds of test for truth.

1. Mathematics and logic (deductive/analytical forms of knowing in which relations are expressed symbolically).
2. Physical science (empirical form of knowing in which truths are tested by observation and experiment).
3. History and the human sciences (forms involving propositions connected with intentions).
4. Literature and fine arts (aesthetic forms).
5. Morals (rationally deduced from a broad base of other understandings).
6. Religion.
7. Philosophy.

An alternative basis for curriculum planning, put forward by Richard Whitfield, uses Phenix's *Realms of Meanings*, 1964, as a theory:

For Phenix, rationality as the distinguishing feature of man is important, but insufficient because of its apparently excessive emphasis on logical cognitive behaviour at the possible expense of the emotions, creativity, and conscience, which are far from being *entirely* cognitive, i.e. ultimately describable purely in terms of language and symbol. He contrasts man's ability to derive meaning and purpose from experiences (though the pathways are rarely smooth) with trends in modern Western society which tend to promote a sense of meaninglessness: the spirit of scepticism and destructive criticism in which the validity of all meanings is brought into question; depersonalization arising from extreme specialization; over-abundance of both knowledge and manufactured products; and rapid social changes which promote insecurity. The curriculum should, according to Phenix, be designed with particular attention to these sources of

Organization of Knowledge

meaninglessness (partly to provide motivation) using the disciplines of knowledge as vehicles. He differentiates six hierarchical *realms of meaning* associated with the disciplines indicated.

Realms of Meaning (Phenix)	Meanings derived from	Disciplines (modified from Phenix)
1 Symbolics	Communication — the necessary means of expressing all meanings.	Ordinary language, logic, mathematics, symbols in expressive arts.
2 Empirics	Truths framed upon the experimentally verified conceptual system.	Physical, life and social sciences including psychology.
3 Aesthetics	Contemplative perception and idealized subjectivities.	Literature, music, visual, and movement arts.
4 Synnoetics (relational insight between other persons and the self)	Interpersonal relationships.	Parts of literature, philosophy, history, psychology and theology.
5 Ethics and Morality	Obligation to codes freely and responsibly selected.	Parts of philosophy and theology.
6 Synoptics	Integrated selfhood.	Philosophy, religion, history

The realms are the general areas of understanding a person requires for adequate functioning within the civilized community and within himself, and they mirror certain undeniable facets of the human species... Through initiation into the realms of meaning by appropriate choices of disciplines, Phenix's 'complete person' appears as one 'skilled in the use of speech, symbol, and gesture; well informed and capable of creating and appreciating objects of aesthetic interest; endowed with a rich and disciplined life in relation to self and others, able to make wise decisions, to judge between right and wrong, and possessed of an integral outlook' (Phenix, p.8). These attributes of the whole person enshrine the aims of a general education. Although Phenix does not rule out some specialization within the curriculum for general education, related to interest and aptitude, he asserts that the curricular task is to provide for learnings in all six of the realms of meaning in terms of which man's nature and conscious experience is defined. 'Without these a person cannot realize his essential humanness. If any one of the six is missing, the person lacks a basic ingredient of experience. They are to the fulfilment of human meanings something like what basic nutrients are to the health of an organism'. (Phenix, p.270).

R. C. WHITFIELD (1971).

Since 1944 there have been a number of attempts to define the secondary curriculum in terms of what everyone needs to know in our society — a common curriculum. It will be useful to examine one well-known example, namely, the HMI document *Curriculum 11-16*, 1977:

Common Needs
Since the majority of pupils leave school at the statutory leaving age, the nature and purposes of the curriculum up to this point must be determined by what we believe sixteen year olds should know, be able to do, and be able to do better at sixteen than they could do at eleven. Pupils and their particular needs and circumstances differ but we believe there are general goals appropriate for all pupils, which have to be translated into curricular objectives in terms of subjects/disciplines/areas of learning activity. If our view is right and more agreement could be reached nationally about these objectives, then the consequences of the diversity of schemes of secondary reorganization and of school population mobility could be mitigated, though clearly not removed. In other words, if agreement about the objectives of teaching, say, history could be reached by national professional consensus, it would be of less consequence that pupils may move from a school where they have studied one period of history to a school in which they will be asked to study a completely different one; discontinuity of syllabus content there will still be, but the pupils should be able to discern more clearly than many of them do at present why they are being asked to study history, and in this respect at least their experience should be consistent. There is a lot to be said for all those concerned with the drawing up and teaching of curricula defining their aims and objectives and trying to think within the context of wider needs, rather than solely with reference to their own circumstances.

Towards a Common Curriculum
What have pupils a reasonable right to expect, given that they are obliged to be in school until they are sixteen? In the first place, without any doubt they have the right to expect to be enabled to take their place in society and in work, and this means that schools must scrutinize their curricula most carefully to see what is being done, by deliberate policies, to meet these expectations. Insofar as pupils may marry at sixteen, vote at eighteen, and become involved in legal responsibilities,

what has the curriculum—the schools' deliberate educational policy done to help them in these matters of fundamental importance to adult life? More than this, even though it may sound somewhat grandly put, pupils are members of a complicated civilization and culture, and it is reasonable to argue that they have nothing less than a right to be introduced to a selection of its essential elements. Options systems may well prevent this from happening: the freedom to stop studying history, or art, or music, or biology at fourteen means that pupils are not being given the introduction to their own cultural inheritance to which we believe they have a right. No one disputes the irrefutable case for basic skills and techniques; equally there is a case for cultural experiences and an introduction to values. There is also just as strong a case—less often acknowledged—for the formation of attitudes to each other, to work, to obligations in society and not least to themselves. For themselves, pupils will need competence and an increasing sense of self-reliance, and the means whereby to develop a sense of integrity in the inevitably changing circumstances that await them.

It is for these reasons that our definition of a common curriculum is broad and makes substantial claims on time. We see that common curriculum as a body of skills, concepts, attitudes and knowledge, to be pursued, to a depth appropriate to their ability, by all pupils in the compulsory years of secondary education for a substantial part of their time, perhaps as much as two-thirds or three-quarters of the total time available. The remainder would be used either to deepen understanding of studies already in hand, or to undertake new activities, or both.

Constructing a Common Curriculum

It is at this point that we come to the heart of our thesis. We see the curriculum to be concerned with introducing pupils during the period of compulsory schooling to certain essential 'areas of experience'. They are listed below in alphabetical order so that no other order of importance may be inferred: in our view, they are equally important.

Checklist

Areas of Experience
The aesthetic and creative
The ethical
The linguistic
The mathematical
The physical

Organization of Knowledge
>   The scientific
>   The social and political
>   The spiritual

FURTHER READING
Paul Hirst's *Knowledge and the Curriculum*, 1974, is a very useful collection of papers, mostly published elsewhere, on various aspects of philosophy and curriculum. Ch. 6 is particularly useful. It includes Hirst, 1965.
For a very different philosophical point of view Richard Pring's *Knowledge and Schooling*, 1976, is extremely readable.

QUESTIONS
1. What kind of theory lies behind the division of the curriculum into eight 'areas of experience'?
2. What are the problems of planning a curriculum on this basis, and carrying it out in the context of a school?

PART TWO
HISTORICAL AND POLITICAL

5
Stability and Change in the Curriculum Peter Gordon

It would be difficult to account for the evolution of our present-day school curriculum merely by cataloguing those great landmarks, the Education Acts. A more fruitful approach would be to examine the relationships existing at various times between education and ideologies, social class and the state of the economy, as well as political, institutional and administrative constraints. Of course, not all these factors would be relevant at any particular time and it is one of the tasks facing the historian to tease out the complex web of interrelating factors underlying curriculum change or which help to account for stability over a period of time.

Before we consider some of the attempts which have been made to achieve this, it is necessary to justify the need for those concerned with curriculum decision-making to have some understanding of the history of the curriculum. In the first place, it helps to account for the present status of 'subjects' in schools, why mathematics has comparatively high status when compared with, say, home economics. As one writer has stated,

> Detailed inquiry into the way the subject matter of different disciplines has accumulated, the balance sought and achieved at different periods, the relation between special and general education and varying arguments in support of different proportions for each—all this leads to a deeper understanding. The student who has studied these developments will be in a better position to plan his own courses, recognize their relation to others, and perceive the educational programme as a whole, its sense and direction. He will also be forewarned against the tendency to justify existing practice on the grounds that it corresponds to certain innate qualities of the child's mind—such, for instance, as the Crowther Committee's claim that grammar schools rightly provide a highly specialized form of education in their sixth forms because children are essentially

'subject-minded'.
B. SIMON, 'The History of Education', in J. W. Tibble, ed., *The Study of Education*, 1966, pp.100-1.

Second, such a study will remind us that the tendency to take for granted the existing status of a subject as being 'fixed' is incorrect and that there are no iron laws in this matter. The fortunes of classics over the last 30 years is a case in point.

Third, by focusing on the evolution of the curriculum and the evidence available, it will be possible to test some hypotheses put forward by sociologists of knowledge — that education is a means of social control and that subject barriers are arbitrary and artificial.

Fourth, the wide-ranging nature of the history of the curriculum raises questions about the nature of schooling and opens up, as will be seen below, new aspects of research which help towards a greater understanding of the process of education in schools.

Some Models of Explanation
There have been a number of attempts made to account for the reasons why curriculum changes.

1. An obvious one would be to list the different factors inolved in the state of the curriculum in a society at any given time. Without being listed in any particular order, the most important ones are perhaps economic and demographic change, pressure groups, religion, the effect of examinations, government policy, political and philosophical considerations. Stuart Maclure, 1970, p.2, has suggested that a model might be constructed which would be useful in studying the effect of changes between these factors in a system. On a vertical axis could be set out the formal, legal and administrative controls which influence the education system and on the horizontal, the professional, academic, social and economic influences. By constructing a grid which looks and acts like a fish net, it would be possible at any one point in time to see the result of existing tensions.

2. Another model concerns itself more directly with the relationship between education and ideologies. The best known example is that of Raymond Williams, 1965, pp.145-76, who examined the effect of nineteenth-century industrial society on democracy. Williams identified three groups who were involved in the debate: the public educators, the industrial trainers and the old humanists, each group viewing education differently. We can trace elements of all three schools of thought in our modern curriculum. The aristocratic or gentry ideology, where curriculum was not geared specifically to education: the *bourgeois* which looked to increasingly specialist curricula for professional purposes: and

the proletarian, which was characterized by practical and vocational subjects. Two 'traditions' in English education, the grammar and the elementary, was largely the outcome. A fourth category, the democratic, which united reformers of all classes, offering a general education through a common curriculum, can now be added. One difficulty in using this model, as Williams himself acknowledged, is that the groups overlapped and reformed in their alliances, so no close correspondence of ideology and social class can be derived.

A somewhat different categorization, also stemming from differing ideologies, was suggested by Ioan Davies, (1969). He proposed four types:

a) *Conservative:* concern here is for maintaining the *status quo* and the need for elements of 'high culture' in curriculum, as expressed by T. S. Eliot, G. H. Bantock and other writers.

b) *Revisionist:* this involves a study of waste of talent in the system, e.g. 11+ and a 'systems' approach. This is an input-output model, which favours the education-occupation link.

c) *Romantic:* the stress on *individual* development and learning, derived from Froebel, Montessori and Piaget, has led to 'progressive' education and considerable reforms in the primary school curriculum.

d) *Democratic-Socialist:* represented by and stemming from nineteenth-century thinkers who sought equal opportunity for all. The political tradition of the Fabians and TUC exemplify this philosophy.

Again, there is some overlap, for instance, social philosophers and writers inhabit both categories a) and b) although representing different traditions. These categories illustrate the ideologies involved in schools adopting the latest knowledge in a particular field.

iii) A comparative approach would involve an examination of *types* of curriculum which are operated in different systems (Bell, 1971, p.18). Diagrammatically, it is possible to represent this scheme as follows

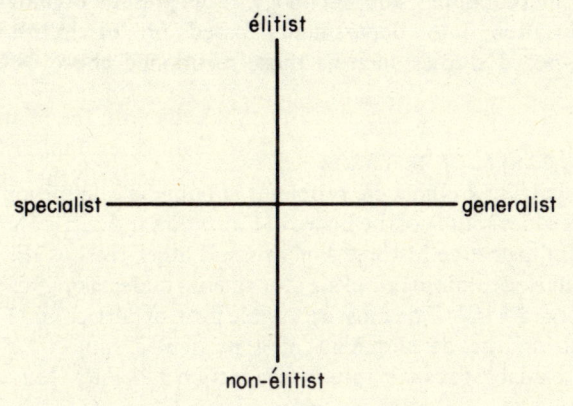

```
                    élitist
                      |
                      |
                      |
   specialist ————————+———————— generalist
                      |
                      |
                      |
                   non-élitist
```

The vertical elitist/non-elitist axis indicates the status of a discipline in a system. The horizontal axis is a representation of the extent to which the discipline is specialist or generalist. Although such a representation does not, of course, explain why curriculum changes, it could be a useful form for analyzing and comparing the histories of different disciplines.

Problems of Historical Research

For anyone undertaking research in the area of the history of the curriculum, there are at least six main problems to be considered:

1. LACK OF BACKGROUND

As the study of the curriculum is itself fairly recent, it is not surprising that there are few books devoted especially to its history. Many of the standard texts on the history of education refer to aspects of curriculum, but this is obviously only one of the topics covered. Equally, there are a number of individual school histories, of varying quality and interest, which deal more specifically with the development of curriculum, but area studies are lacking. Most histories of School Boards deal largely with political and administrative aspects.

2. NEED FOR INTERDISCIPLINARITY

The study of the history of curriculum, as will now be clear, is a complex one and requires a wide range of skills and the acquaintance with more than one discipline. Ideally, such research should be undertaken by a team of people with complementary interests. For example, a study of childhood and the curriculum demands a knowledge of psychology as well as history; the effects of utilitarianism on the curriculum can best be understood if the student has a philosophic background; and the relationship between industrialization and the curriculum requires a grounding in economics and sociology. The present organization of higher education into departments based on disciplines makes across-the-board studies such as those mentioned above difficult to undertake.

3. CHOOSING AREAS OF RESEARCH

Following on from 2., there are problems of boundary definition. When, for example, does a study of the Board of Education and curriculum policy become administrative history? For this and other reasons the student would be advised to adopt one of six strategies in undertaking research:

    a) *Subject or Phase* — The most accessible form of curriculum history is that of tracing the development of a particular subject. Abundant material is available for such a study (see section 4. below). This could be either in conjunction with or separate from a consideration of some phase, e.g. language in the primary school, secondary school science.

b) *Introduction of New Subjects* — Although similar to a), it differs in providing a case-study approach to how and why changes in the curriculum take place. Examples would be the introduction of moral education and the rise of social science teaching in schools.

c) *Issues* — The focus here would be on certain key events which have significance for curriculum development. The study by John White on the possible reasons behind the freeing of the elementary curriculum from 1926, 'The End of the Compulsory Curriculum', in *The Curriculum. The Doris Lee Lectures*, University of London Institute of Education, 1977, pp.22-39, is a good example of this approach.

d) *Interrelatedness* — The interest under this heading would be in investigating the evolution of teaching practices, methods and philosophies on curriculum. Family grouping in primary schools, the emergence of middle schools, the effect of architectural rethinking, particularly in the form of open plan buildings, integrated studies, multi-cultural education are other examples.

e) *Span of Time* — This would involve a consideration of the whole curriculum over a period of time at a given level where important changes can be identified; for example, the rise of the New Education movement in the inter-war period. In such a study, it is advisable to choose a limited period of time if the study is to be manageable.

4. AVAILABILITY OF SOURCES

One of the main difficulties in embarking on such a study is the superabundance of *printed materials* available. Some indication of this richness is given in the final section of this chapter. The nineteenth century was the age of royal commissions, select committees, printed reports, journals, pamphleteers and associations, and education is well-represented. How to select and retrieve the relevant literature is a problem which modern bibliographical techniques are helping to overcome.

The use of *archive materials*, although equally abundant, presents more difficulties. Few depositories, at national, county or local levels, have as yet indexed their holdings under 'curriculum'. This can lead to the expenditure of considerable time by the researcher in tracing relevant and meaningful references. It should also be borne in mind that the nearer the study comes to the present time, the more sensitive the archive material becomes. Post-war studies of Government and DES policy-making in relation to curriculum and local education authority attitudes towards aspects of comprehensive schools relevant to such a study present this sort of difficulty.

5. INTERPRETATION OF MATERIALS

Nowadays there are a number of different interpretations of historical material, not confined to that of curriculum alone. Philip McCann has pointed out that the traditional orientation of educational history has been mainly descriptive and empirical, largely concentrating on the upper and intermediate levels — universities, public and secondary schools; popular education has largely been treated from an administrative point of view. McCann (1977, pp.x-xi) states that popular education should be examined as a social process,

> an interaction between the aims of the ruling interests and the determination of the working class to construct a meaningful social existence. Historians have often tended to confuse the aim with its fulfilment and educational historians in particular have assumed that what schools set out to do was achieved without taking into account the problematic nature of the response of the working-class pupil and his parents.

This view of education as a means of social control, promoted by Marx, Gramsci and others, is opposed to a more functionalist view of education of society. The formulation of hypotheses in studies of the curriculum are essential but a polarization of approaches, given the paucity of evidence for arriving at firm conclusions at the present time, should be avoided.

One other important problem is the interpretation of nineteenth-century data. On the quantitative side we know, for instance, that the census returns of 1870 relating to the provision of elementary school accommodation before school boards were established, were incorrectly computed. In addition, lacking a national classification of social class occupations, definitions and descriptions differed according to the group or individual making the identification. However, it must be realized that such problems of interpretation inevitably belong to the field of history generally.

6. AVAILABLE TECHNIQUES

As we have seen in 2. above, curriculum history calls for a multidisciplinary approach; one problem is the selection of techniques to carry out a study. Besides the obvious *historical* tool of knowledge based on primary and secondary sources, there are other disciplines which offer useful techniques.

One of the oldest tools of sociology has been the comparative method. Marten Shipman's *Modernisation and Education*, Faber, 1971, examines British and Japanese education in a socio-historical context. The effects of bureaucracy, derived from Max Weber and others, are studied by F.

Musgrove, *Patterns of Power and Authority in English Education*, Methuen, 1971, Ch. 7, pp.88-105. The views contained in S. Bowles and H. Gintis, *Schooling in Capitalist America: Education Reform and the Contradictions of Economic Life*, Basic Books, 1976, which examines the relationship between capitalism and schooling, could be compared with the British situation.

Geographical techniques have reminded us of the spatial element in the study of education. The consequences of catchment zones defined by social areas for schooling have always been important. The physical location of schools can be correlated with success measured in academic terms, such as scholarship awards at 11 years of age; population density and elementary school status can also be plotted. (See W. E. Marsden, 'Education and the Social Geography of Nineteenth Century Towns and Cities', in D. A. Reeder, ed., *Urban Education in the Nineteenth Century*, Taylor and Francis, 1977, pp.49-73.)

Besides using techniques drawn from disciplines, the researcher can employ ideas drawn from other areas. The notions of intelligence, as expressed by psychologists during the past century, have affected what should be taught. Definitions of citizenship, community and the relation between the individual and the state, as defined by philosophers from the last quarter of the nineteenth century, suggest further lines of approach to the study of curriculum. Finally, mention should be made of studies in political science and educational administration which are helpful in an investigation of the politics of the curriculum, e.g. R. Barker, *Education and Politics 1900-51*, Oxford University Press, 1972, and M. Kogan, *The Politics of Educational Change*, Manchester University Press, 1978.

SOURCES

In the brief guide to sources for curriculum history which follows, a selection has had to be made from the large corpus of materials available.

G. Kitson Clark's *Guide for Research Students Working on Historical Subjects*, Cambridge University Press, 1972 edition, is a useful starting point.

a) *Bibliographies* include

    M. Humby, *A Guide to the Literature of Education: Education Libraries Bulletin, Supplement I*, University of London Institute of Education 3rd edition, 1975;

    W. B. Stephens, *Sources For English Local History*, Manchester University Press, 1973, Ch. VII, 'Education', pp.131-63;

    G. Baron, *A Bibliographical Guide to the English Education System*, Athlone Press, 1965;

    C. W. J. Higson's *Sources for the History of Education*, 1967, and *Supplement to Sources for the History of Education*, 1976, Library

Stability and Change in the Curriculum

    Association, identify university libraries where items can be consulted. The most comprehensive coverage is the *British Educational Index*, Library Association, August 1954 onwards, and it contains an alphabetical index of subjects.
b) For background reading on the history of education see W. H. G. Armytage, *Four Hundred Years of Education*, Cambridge University Press, 1965, and the three volumes by B. Simon, *Studies in the History of Education 1780-1870*, 1960, *Education and the Labour Movement 1870-1920*, 1965, and *The Politics of Educational Reform 1920-40*, 1974, all Lawrence and Wishart.
    R. L. Archer, *Secondary Education in the Nineteenth Century*, (originally Cambridge University Press, 1921), reprinted by Frank Cass, 1966, J. Lawson and H. Silver, *A Social History of Education*, Methuen, 1973, and H. C. Barnard, *A History of English Education from 1760*, University of London Press, 2nd edition, 1961.
c) On the history of school curriculum see the following:
    R. D. Bramwell, *Elementary School Work, 1900-1925*, University of Durham Institute of Education, 1951;
    J. M. Goldstrom, *The Social Content of Education 1808-1870*, Irish University Press, 1972;
    P. Gordon and D. Lawton, *Curriculum Change in the Nineteenth and Twentieth Centuries*, Hodder and Stoughton, 1978;
    P. H. J. H. Gosden, *How They Were Taught*, Blackwell, 1969;
    P. W. Musgrave, ed., *Sociology, History and Education*, Methuen, 1970, and Foster Watson, *The Old Grammar Schools*, Cambridge University Press, 1916, reprinted by Frank Cass, 1968.
d) There are numerous biographies of educationists, but two key works should be consulted:
The Compact Edition of the Dictionary of National Biography, Oxford University Press, 1975, is complete up to 1960 and contains an alphabetical index; and Ann Christophers, *An Index to Nineteenth Century British Educational Biography. Education Libraries Bulletin Supplement 10*, University of London Institute of Education, 1965.
e) Short articles on aspects of curriculum are to be found in various journals, particularly the *British Journal of Educational Studies*, 1952-, *Durham Research Review*, 1950-, *Educational Review*, 1948-, *History of Education* 1972-, *Journal of Educational Administration and History*, 1968-. The *British Journal of Educational Studies* has, over the years, published bibliographical articles on such topics as teacher training, handicapped children, technical education and grammar schools.
    Many other journals occasionally include relevant articles, see, for example, the *British Journal of Sociology*, the *Journal of Curriculum*

Studies, Past and Present and *Victorian Studies*.

f) In using official papers, it is advisable to read first M. Argles, *British Government Publications in Education in the Nineteenth Century. Guides to the Sources in the History of Education No. 1*, History of Education Society, 1971, and P. Ford, *A Guide to Parliamentary Papers: What They Are, How to Find Them, How to Use Them*, Irish University Press, 3rd edition, 1972.

Most of the major royal commissions in the nineteenth century dealt with important aspects of curriculum: for secondary schools, see Clarendon, 1864, Taunton, 1868, and Bryce, 1895; for elementary see Cross, 1888, and for technical education, Devonshire, 1875, and Samuelson, 1884.

In the present century, reports of Consultative Committees such as Hadow, 1926, 1931 and 1933, and Central Advisory Councils, particularly Crowther, 1959, Newsom, 1963, and Plowden, 1967, should be consulted.

The Annual Minutes and Reports of the Committee of Council on Education, 1838-98, contain detailed information on the day-to-day running of schools; from 1899, when the Board of Education was established, the Reports become more general in character. The *Report for the Year 1910-11*, HMSO, 1912, gives a good summary of the development of curriculum from 1862 to 1911, pp.5-41.

An exhaustive survey of curriculum in Britain and abroad was carried out by the Office of Special Inquiries and Reports, a branch of the Education Department established in 1895. Between 1897 and 1914, the Office published twenty-eight volumes under the title *Special Reports on Educational Subjects*, HMSO, referred to as the Sadler Reports after its first Director.

The official Annual Codes issued by the Education Department stipulated curriculum requirements. From the beginning of the present century the policy implications of educational decisions have been disseminated by means of Circulars. Many have direct bearing on curriculum and can be located in J. E. Vaughan, *Board of Education Circulars: A Finding List and Index. Guide to the Sources in the History of Education No. 2*, History of Education Society, 1972. The *Handbooks of Suggestions for Teachers*, issued from 1905 until the outbreak of the Second World War are valuable texts. Since the establishment of the Board of Education, official Education Pamphlets (numbered) on different subject areas usually begin with a historical chapter. For example, the Ministry of Education Pamphlet No. 38, *Science in Secondary Schools*, HMSO, 1960, devotes 27 pages to the development of science teaching from 1860 to 1960.

Reactions to official pronouncements can be followed in the

volumes of Hansard's *Parliamentary Debates in the House of Commons*. There are five series since publication began: 1st series, 1803-20, 2nd series, 1820-30, 3rd series, 1830-51, 4th series, 1852-1908, 5th series, 1909 onwards.

g) Influences on the curriculum, as noted earlier, come from a variety of sources. Mention should be made of a few of them. *Foreign* influences can be traced in W. H. G. Armytage's three volumes, *The American Influence on English Education*, 1967, *The French Influence on English Education*, 1968, and *The German Influence on English Education*, 1969, all Routledge and Kegan Paul.

Administrative influences are described in G. Sutherland, *Policy-Making in Elementary Education, 1870-1895*, Oxford University Press, 1973, and sources are given in P. H. J. H. Gosden, *Educational Administration; A Biographical Guide*, University of Leeds Institute of Education, 1967. For *architectural* influences, see M. Seaborne, *The English School. Its Architecture and Organization, Vol. I 1370-1870*, 1971, and M. Seaborne and R Lowe, *Vol. II, 1870-1977*, 1977, both Routledge and Kegan Paul.

Political influences are set out in I. G. K. Fenwick, *The Comprehensive School 1944-70*, Methuen, 1976, and M. Kogan, *The Politics of Education*, Penguin, 1971.

h) Finally, for research which requires the use of archival sources, there is a full list of addresses of national, county and local holders in The Royal Commission on Historical Manuscripts, *Record Repositories in Great Britain*, HMSO, 6th edition, 1979. Most record offices have either manuscript lists or index cards of education deposits, although there is no standard method of classification.

Two excellent publications are A. Black, *Guide to Education Records in the County Record Office Cambridge*, Cambridgeshire and Isle of Ely County Council, 1977, and C. R. Davey, ed., *Education in Hampshire and the Isle of Wight*, Hampshire Archivists' Group Publication No. 3, 1972. Published teaching units, consisting of copies of original documents, printed reports and illustrations, can be a valuable introduction to archive work. Of particular interest are the Department of Education and Science unit, *Education Act 1870*, 1970, the University of Newcastle-upon-Tyne Department of Education Archive Teaching Unit No. 4, *Popular Education 1700-1870*, 1969, and the Essex Record Office, Seax Series of Teaching Portfolios No. 6, *Education in Essex c. 1710-1910*, Essex Record Office, 1974.

FURTHER READING

A good volume of essays with readings is P. Nash, ed., *History and Education. The Educational Uses of the Past*, Random House, New York,

Stability and Change in the Curriculum

1970. For a brief guide to literature on nineteenth-century elementary, secondary, scientific and technical education, see G. Sutherland, ed., *Education in 19th Century Britain*, Irish Academic Press, 1978. Further suggestions for approaches to the history of the curriculum are contained in Asa Briggs' 'The Study of the History of Education', *History of Education*, Vol. 1, No. 1, January, 1972, and P. Gordon, 'Commitments and Developments in the Elementary School Curriculum, 1870-1907', *History of Education*, Vol. 6, No. 1, February 1977.

QUESTIONS
1. How satisfactory as explanations of curriculum change are the models described in this chapter?
2. The history of the curriculum is said to be 'history written from above'. Is there an alternative?

6
Concepts of Childhood and The Curriculum
Peter Gordon

Although historians and educationists are showing considerable interest in the evolution of the concept of childhood, there are a number of different interpretations which make generalizations difficult, as will be explained later. However, an outline of historical changes in this country is first of all necessary.

Middle Ages to Sixteenth Century
Up to the sixteenth century in England, statutes stipulated that poor children should be put out to work early. For the upper classes, children were sent away from home at an early age to act as pages and maids for other noble households and received whatever counted as education there. Similarly, for the middle classes, company (guild) regulations forbade the apprenticing of sons to fathers. An anonymous Italian observer of the English scene in the late fifteenth century wrote:

> The want of affection in the English is strongly manifested towards their children; for after having kept them at home till they arrive at the age of seven or nine years at the utmost, they put them out, both males and females, to hard service in the houses of other people, binding them generally for another seven or nine years. And these are called apprentices, and during that time they perform all the most menial offices: and few are born who are exempted from this fate; for everyone, however rich he may be, sends away his children to the houses of others, whilst he in return, receives those of strangers in his. And on inquiring their reason for this severity, they answered that they did it in order that their children might have better manners. But I, for my part, believe that they do it because they like to enjoy all their comforts themselves, and that they are better served by strangers than they would be by their own children. Besides which, the English being great epicures, and very avaricious by nature, indulge in the most delicate fare themselves and give their household the coarsest bread, and beer,

Concepts of Childhood and the Curriculum

and cold meat baked on Sunday for the week, which, however, they allow them in great abundance. That if they had their children at home, they would be obliged to give them the same food as they made use for themselves.

A Relation, or rather a true account of the Island of England, trs. G. A. Sneyd, 1847, pp.24-5.

Ariès claims that in the Middle Ages, the family unit as such did not exist: instead, the child, a miniature adult, was part of an 'extended' family whose main function was to advance its own position through marriage and property:

> In medieval society the idea of childhood did not exist; this is not to suggest that children were neglected, forsaken or despised. The idea of childhood is not to be confused with affection for children: it corresponds to an awareness of the particular nature of childhood, that particular nature which distinguishes the child from the adult, even the young adult. In medieval society this awareness was lacking. That is why, as soon as the child could live without the constant solicitude of his mother, his nanny or his cradle-rocker, he belonged to adult society. That adult society now strikes us as rather puerile: no doubt this is largely a matter of mental age, but it is also due to its physical age, because it was partly made up of children and youths. Language did not give the word 'child' the restricted meaning we give it today: people said 'child' much as we say 'lad' in everyday speech. The absence of definition extended to every sort of social activity: games, crafts, arms. There is not a single collective picture of the times in which children are not to be found, nestling singly or in pairs in the trousse hung round women's necks, or urinating in a corner, or playing their part in a traditional festival, or as apprentices in a workshop, or as pages serving a knight, etc.

P. ARIÈS, *Centuries of Childhood*, 1962, p.128.

Great changes came about during the period 1540 to 1600 through two forces: humanism and the desire to preserve a fixed social hierarchy. Lawrence Stone (1965) has described well the effect of these changes. Italian humanism was mediated through educational reformers such as Colet and Erasmus who induced the nobility and gentry to give a more intellectual training to their children. There was also the threat to key positions in society with the rise to power of men of low birth, such as Wolsey and Cromwell, which stimulated the nobles to become acquainted with law, writing and foreign languages in order to maintain

Concepts of Childhood and the Curriculum

their position.

> In this first, heroic, phase of the educational revolution, peers and gentry possessed an enthusiasm for pure scholarship that far outran the practical needs of an administrative *élite*. They rushed headlong into a course of study that stands comparison with that of any educational system of twentieth-century Europe. Men like Elyot were well aware that their purpose was to train a governing class, but they tended to exaggerate the academic side of the programme. Elyot himself advised a study of Greek and Latin literature from the ages of 7 to 13, followed by a university course of logic, rhetoric, cosmography, and history, though he admitted the need for physical recreation to strengthen the body. Parents were won over by these ideas, and men like the 4th Duke of Norfolk, the 8th Earl of Essex under Elizabeth, and Sir William Wentworth and the 9th Earl of Northumberland in the early seventeenth century, all urged upon their children the importance of a social academic education in the classics, logic and rhetoric, science, modern languages, and the common law. In his enthusiasm Sir Henry Slingsby began to teach his son Latin (by Montaigne's method) at the age of four. In 1632 Sir John Strode told his son that 'learning to be a gentleman is like a diamond set in a gold ring: one doth beautify the other', and Richard Evelyn successfully instilled into the mind of his son John the notion that it is 'better to be unborn than untaught'. Here is learning exalted not merely as a means to virtue and public service, but as an end in itself.
>
> L. STONE, *The Crisis of the Aristocracy 1558-1641*, 1965, pp.676-7.

No one pattern of formal schooling can be discerned to meet this new demand. By the seventeenth century, the practice of educating children in a noble household had virtually ceased. Children (including girls) were often tutored at home up to the age of about 14. Local 'grammar' schools were used by a range of social classes, though gradually the aristocracy became identified with fashionable boarding schools in or around London. As early as 1570, Richard Mulcaster, the first headmaster of Merchant Taylors' School, in his book *Elementaire*, complained of 'the rich aping the custom of Princes' in having private tutors for their boys and withdrawing them from these schools. Elementary and free schools existed in considerable number at this time. Elizabethans were keen advocates of girls' education, Mulcaster himself declaring 'myself am for them tooth and nail'.

Late Seventeenth Century

So far, religious elements of childhood had not been widely stressed, but

Concepts of Childhood and the Curriculum

from the seventeenth century onwards, primers, aimed at both parents and children, appeared which stressed the virtues of morality, honesty and hard work, the latter in the form of long school hours. Not surprisingly the emergence of the Protestant middle classes, at this time, gave rise to what has been called the 'Protestant ethic'. The publication of books containing lists of psalms to be learnt and how to behave in church was backed up by beatings both at home and in school. Reflecting on the upbringing of her own family, John Wesley's mother, Susannah, said of her babies 'When turned a year old (and some before), they were taught to fear the rod, and to cry softly', (quoted in de Mause, 1974, p.41).

After the Restoration, with an easing of attitudes, it is possible to detect a more enlightened view of childhood. In his influential book, *Some Thoughts Concerning Education*, published in 1682, John Locke condemned beating in the following terms:

> A gentle persuasion and reasoning with children will most times do much better. You will perhaps wonder to find me mention reasoning with children, and yet I cannot but think that the true way of dealing with them. They understand it as early as they do language, and if I misobserve not they have to be treated as rational creatures sooner than is imagined.

1880 edn., p.60.

Eighteenth Century

Along with this sentiment, the appeal to reason continued the notion of the child as an adult writ small. Special dress for school children only began to appear at the end of the eighteenth century and they were expected to think as adults from an early age (thus the uncompromising nature of school textbooks of this time). In 1741, Lord Chesterfield wrote to his son,

> This is the last letter I shall write to you as a little boy, for tomorrow you will attain your ninth year, so that for the future I shall treat you as a youth. You must now commence a different course of life, a different course of studies. No more levity. Childish toys and playthings must be thrown aside, and your mind directed to serious objects. What was not unbecoming to a child would be disgraceful to a youth.

I. PINCHBECK and M. HEWITT, *Children in English Society*, 1968, Vol. 1, p.298.

The distancing of parents (and teachers) from children was at least partly

Concepts of Childhood and the Curriculum

understandable when the rate of infant mortality is considered. It has been calculated that in 1750, three-quarters of children christened in London had died before the age of five. But social changes were taking place which were altering the nature of the family. The increasing wealth of middle and upper class families during the eighteenth century led to a desire for more comfortable living conditions. No longer did the family exist in its extended form. Architecturally, houses were built which separated off servants and which assisted in strengthening the family psychologically as a unit. It is interesting to note that this led to an opposing tendency. A room, or rooms, were set aside for children and during the eighteenth century, the nursery became increasingly common, beginning to double also as the schoolroom. By the 1840s, the Victorian nursery had developed, together with the nanny: the separation of mother and children was then more complete than before. See J. Gathorne Hardy, *The Rise and Fall of the British Nanny*, 1972, Chapter 8.

It was in such a climate that Rousseau's *Emile* (1762) was favourably received. That children should be free in an unspecified way was an important point. Rousseau's advocacy of breast feeding rather than wetnursing was a landmark in intellectual history and gave the stamp to a movement which was already under way. A retired teacher in Limoges in 1808 described how things had changed since his own grim childhood, with mothers and infants now beaming at each other, the nursery radiant with smiles.

> Cheered up and embraced without end, (the children) will remain unknowing of ill will. Completely unconstrained in their clean sheets and well cared for, their beautiful little bodies develop rapidly. They need merely be of good humour and good health, and they'll draw the eyes of all who come near.
>
> Quoted in E. SHORTER, *The Making of the Modern Family*, 1976, p.191.

Such descriptions, of course, are confined to middle class families. For the poor, labour rather than education was considered more appropriate, either in the house, the field or the factory. These classes have left us with little or no evidence of their views of childhood from this time.

Nineteenth and Twentieth Centuries
By the nineteenth century, there was a dramatic shift in societal views of childhood. Of these, perhaps the most significant was in the sphere of *children's rights*. Up to this time, parents were free to punish, apprentice off and abandon children almost at will. Children were held to be legally

responsible at seven and public hanging at this age (and less) continued into the nineteenth century. Hours in factories were unregulated and educational provision was unspecified. Philanthropic endeavour by individuals brought about the Factory Acts in 1819 and 1833, the latter of which made illegal the employment of children under nine years of age and required employers to provide two hours schooling per day. Even the oppressive Poor Law Act of 1834, which separated children from their parents, stipulated that suitable education should be available within the workhouses. Sir James Kay-Shuttleworth, (then Dr James Kay) at that time an Assistant Poor Law Commissioner, started his educational experiments in one of these institutions at Norwood before becoming the first Secretary of the Privy Council Committee of Council on Education in 1839. Schooling, however, was generally considered to be an instrument for reforming children and the curriculum reflected this attitude.

The 1860s onwards witnessed a flurry of activity aimed at securing better treatment for children. The Society for the Prevention of Cruelty to Children, for instance, sprang from a meeting in 1882 organized by the Society for the Prevention of Cruelty to Animals at which the main item of business was the establishment of a dog's home. A Prevention of Cruelty Act passed in 1889, commonly known as the Children's Charter, was one consequence of this campaign, which continued into the present century. The age of consent was raised to 16 only in 1929 and four years previously a father's absolute right over his children was replaced by the equal rights of both parents. The series of Education Acts from 1870 also mirrors these changing attitudes.

Another aspect of this concern is seen in the attention given to children's *physical and welfare* needs, through voluntary bodies such as the Charity Organisation Society, who conducted investigations with the British Medical Association from 1889 into the physical condition of London school children, but official acknowledgement was also given. The published correspondence between J. G. Fitch and Dr J. Crichton-Browne, Superintendent of the West Riding Lunatic Asylum, aired the controversy over overpressure and underfeeding. (Parliamentary Papers 1884, lxi) The result of the inquiry by the Women Inspectors of the Board of Education into Infant Education was another manifestation of the new view of children in relation to the curriculum. (*Reports on Children under Five Years of Age in Public Elementary Schools*, Cd. 2726, 1905.) Sir John Gorst, who had been Minister of Education from 1895 to 1902 in Lord Salisbury's government, in a book written after his retirement and entitled *The Children of the Nation. How Their Health and Vigour Should be Promoted by the State*, 1906, advocated medical inspection and attention to hygiene, more enlightened infant schools, the provision of

Concepts of Childhood and the Curriculum

playgrounds, and healthier school buildings. In the same year, the Education (Provision of Meals) Act came into force. This wider view of curriculum can be contrasted with that enshrined in the earlier Education Codes.

It was only in such a climate that the *ideas of educational reformers* such as Froebel and Pestalozzi could flourish and that the inter-war movement under the banner of the New Educational Fellowship could gather momentum. The *academic study of education*, from the 1880s, child psychology in particular, had influenced thinking.

Three examples will show how attitudes were changing. Dewey wrote in 1916,

> Our tendency to take immaturity as mere lack, and growth as something which fills up the gap between the immature and the mature is due to regarding childhood *comparatively*, instead of intrinsically. We treat it simply as a privation because we are measuring it by adulthood as a fixed standard. This fixes attention upon what the child has not, and will not have till he becomes a man. This comparative standpoint is legitimate enough for some purposes, but if we make it final, the question arises whether we are not guilty of an overweening presumption. Children, if they could express themselves articulately and sincerely, would tell a different tale; and there is excellent adult authority for the conviction that for certain moral and intellectual purposes adults must behave as little children.

J. DEWEY, *Democracy and Education*, 1916, pp.49-50.

Dewey advocated therefore 'plasticity' or the power to learn from experience which leads to the formation of habits.

> Active habits involve thought, invention and initiative in applying capacities to new aims. They are opposed to routine which marks an arrest of growth. Since growth is characteristic of life, education is all one with growing: it has no end beyond itself. The criterion of the value of school education is the extent in which it creates a desire for continued growth and supplies means for making the desire effective in fact.

ibid,. p.62

Percy Nunn, a former Director of the University of London Institute of Education, advanced the argument in his book *Education: Its Data and First Principles* (1920), by emphasizing the creative activity of childhood as expressed in play. In a chapter entitled 'The "Play-Way" in Education' (Ch. 8), Nunn states that

Concepts of Childhood and the Curriculum

It is hardly extravagant to say that in the understanding of play lies the key to most of the practical problems of education. For play, taken in the narrower sense as a phenomena belonging especially to childhood, shows the creative impulses in their clearest, most vigorous and most typical form. Hence it is not essentially creative activities such as art and craftmanship, and, in a smaller measure, geographical exploration and scientific discovery, are felt to have a peculiar affinity with play and are, in fact continuous with it in the development of individuality. Even recreative play and relaxation are misunderstood if viewed merely as attempts to escape from the burden and grind of real life. Whether the player be child or man, they express the external craving of the organism for free self-assertion — a craving that must somehow be fed or the soul would die. All truly effective reform, within education and society, is motivated by the desire to enlarge as much as possible the field in which that central function of life may find worthy and satisfying exercise.

P. NUNN, *Education: Its Data and First Principles*, 1920, p.89.

By 1936, Marie Montessori had proposed that accepted views of childhood needed to be revised: the task of the teacher should be to discover the true child and effect his or her liberation:

We must face the startling fact that the child has a psychic life of which the delicate manifestations pass unperceived, and of which the adult may inadequately mar the pattern or hinder the development.

The adult's environment is not a life-giving accumulation of obstacles leading him to a creation of defences, to deforming efforts at adaptation or else leaving him the victim of suggestion. It is the outward aspect he thus presents that has been considered in the study of child psychology, and it is from this that his characteristics have been defined, as a basis for education. Child psychology is thus something that must be *radically revised*. As we have seen, behind every surprising response on the part of the child, lies an enigma to be deciphered; every form of naughtiness is the outward expression of some deep-centred cause, which cannot be interpreted as the superficial, defensive clash with an unsuitable environment, but as expressing a higher esssential characteristic seeking manifestation. It is as though a storm were hindering the child's soul from coming forth from its secret hiding place, to show itself in the outer world.

M. MONTESSORI, *The Secret of Childhood*, 1936, p.125.

Few of these changes would have come about without *demographic* and *economic influences.* Frank Musgrove (1964) has noted that

> the rising status of the young in the Western World, measured by the protective provision and welfare facilities increasingly at their disposal, has been attributed at least in part to their diminishing proportion of the total population.

Certainly, as the chances of survival increased during the nineteenth century, children came to be more cherished. Musgrove points out that children were of less financial value to parents as the century progressed. This can be attributed to a number of changes which took place in the economy. The Factory Acts were an increasing threat to their earning power: as an insurance against old age for parents, children were less important as the friendly society movement spread: the high survival rate of adolescents by the last 20 years of the nineteenth century resulted in a superabundance of potential labour which was a contributory reason to compulsory education being imposed in 1870 and 1880. In addition, child labour was needed less with the mechanization of industry. Since the 1920s children have been born into an economy in which technological change has led to an upgrading of occupations and a decrease in the proportion of labouring jobs. This, in turn, has been accompanied by an ever-rising school leaving age, which now includes a sizeable proportion of young adults.

The argument has moved, in an age of common schooling and where social class differences between types of schools within the state system have less force, to a consideration of types of curricula most appropriate to the situation.

Tapper (1971) observed in a study of comprehensive schools, that the social class of pupils seemed to be of less consequence in the formation of role aspirations than in grammar schools. Similarly, second stream pupils had higher aspirations than at secondary modern schools. Comprehensive schools are able to ameliorate social class difficulties and thus ease some of the students' difficulties in an educational context. Unfortunately the problem of the non-achiever still remains and newer types of schools have not been particularly successful in tackling it.

Two other facets of the changing concept of childhood are relevant to the nature of school curriculum: the first relates to the status of women, the second concerns the discovery of 'adolescence'. The eighteenth and early nineteenth-century view of middle class girls' education was essentially that of preparation for marriage and home-making. This philosophy was continued into elementary education, where, for example, girls were allowed to substitute sewing for arithmetic. Two official surveys during the present century—the *Report of the*

Concepts of Childhood and the Curriculum

Consultative Committee on the Curriculum of Boys and Girls HMSO, 1923, and the Department of Education and Science, *Curricular Differences for Boys and Girls,* Education Survey No. 21, HMSO, 1975, indicate that there is a lag between officially accepted views and what is practised. views and what is practised.

Although nineteenth-century society expressed concern about street gang members and delinquents, no collective name was given to identify and describe such groups. In the second decade of the present century, G. Stanley Hall (1844-1924), an American psychologist, advanced a theory of adolescence in its own right. In a two-volume work, *Adolescence,* 1916, Hall identified adolescence, lasting from puberty to between the 22nd and 25th years, as a period of 'storm and stress'. Hall's theory of 'recapitulation' stated that the characteristics of a certain age in the development of an individual correspond to some primitive historical stage in the development of the human race. Adolescence, according to Hall, corresponded with the idealism expressed at the beginning of the eighteenth century by such writers as Goethe and Schiller, and is characterized by turbulence, commitment to goals, revolution against the old, expression of personal feelings and need for solitude. One critic of this view is another American psychologist, Albert Bandura, who examined the sources of what he calls 'adolescent mythology' and, based on a study of middle-class families of adolescent boys, concluded:

> If a society labels its adolescents as 'teen-agers', and expects them to be rebellious, unpredictable, sloppy, and wild in their behaviour, and if this picture is repeatedly reinforced by the mass media, such cultural expectations may very well force adolescents into the role of rebel. In this way, a false expectation may serve to instigate and maintain certain role behaviours, in turn, then reinforce the originally false belief. In discussing our research findings with parents' groups I have often been struck by the fact that most parents who are experiencing positive and rewarding relationships with their preadolescent children are, nevertheless, waiting apprehensively and bracing themselves for the stormy adolescent period. Such vigilance can very easily create a small turbulence at least. When the prophesied storm fails to materialize, many parents begin to entertain doubts about the normality of their youngster's social development.

A. BANDURA, 'The Stormy Decade: Fact or Fiction?', in R. E. Muuss (ed) *Adolescent Behaviour and Society, A Book of Readings,* 1975, pp.32-3.

Problems of Interpretation
Much of present-day interpretation of the history of childhood derives

from the work of Philip Ariès in the 1960s. Ariès' views have been disseminated in the United States by Lloyd de Mause and his co-workers, who have developed a psychogenic view of history. The central force for change, it is claimed, is neither economics nor technology, but the 'psychogenic' changes in personality occurring because of successive generations of parent-child interactions. De Mause puts forward five hypotheses which can be tested with reference to historical evidence:

1. That the evolution of parent-child relations constitutes an independent source of historical change. The origin of this evolution lies in the ability of successive generations of parents to regress to the psychic age of their children and work through the anxieties of that age in a better manner the second time they encounter them than they did during their own childhood. The process is similar to that of psychoanalysis, which also involves regression and a second chance to face childhood anxieties.
2. That this 'generational pressure' for psychic change is not only spontaneous, originating in the adult's need to regress and in the child's striving for relationship, but also occurs independent of social and technological change. It therefore can be found even in periods of social and technological stagnation.
3. That the history of childhood is a series of closer approaches between adult and child, with each closing of psychic distance producing fresh anxiety. The reduction of this adult anxiety is the main source of the child-rearing practices of each age.
4. That the obverse of the hypothesis that history involves a general improvement in child care is that the further back one goes in history, the less effective parents are in meeting the developing needs of the child. This would indicate, for instance, that if today in America there are less than a million abused children, there would be a point back in history where most children were what we would now consider abused.
5. That because psychic structure must always be passed from generation to generation through the narrow funnel of childhood, a society's child-rearing practices are not just one item in a list of cultural traits. They are the very condition for the transmission and development of all other cultural elements, and place definite limits on what can be achieved in all other spheres of history. Specific childhood experiences must occur to sustain specific cultural traits, and once these experiences no longer occur the trait disappears.

L. de MAUSE, ed., *The History of Childhood*, 1974, p.3.

De Mause identifies six modes of child-rearing during the course of history. First, there was the *Infanticidal mode* (antiquity to fourth century AD), when parents resolved their anxieties about taking care of their children by killing them. During the *Abandonment mode* (fourth to thirteenth centuries AD), parental recognition of children having souls led to abandonment by fostering or serving in other households. The *Ambivalent mode* (fourteenth to seventeenth centuries) was the time when children entered in their parents' emotional life and therefore had to be moulded or beaten into shape. By the time of the *Intrusive mode* (eighteenth century), the child was no longer a dangerous projection and so punishment diminished; but greater attempts were made to conquer the child's mind by threats of guilt. This was the age of mothers nursing their children. The *Socialization mode* (nineteenth to mid-twentieth centuries), where the raising of a child was now a process of socialization rather than training, de Mause notes, is the source of all twentieth-century psychological models from Freud to Skinner. Conformism was expressed in terms of sociological functionalism. For the first time the father begins to take a direct interest in child-rearing. Finally, there is the *Helping mode* (mid-twentieth century onwards), where the child knows better than the parents what his or her needs are and the parents see their task as helping children to fulfil them. When the child is punished or chastised, apologies by the parent follow. This mode involves enormous expenditure of time and energy on the part of parents and few have been able to attempt consistently this kind of child care.

This approach has been criticized by other researchers such as Peter Laslett, Director of the Cambridge Group for the History of Population and Social Structure. Laslett notes that for the distant past, the child appears in written records far less frequently than would be expected. In medieval times, books tended to repeat each other in their authorities and the investigator would need to understand the sources in their original languages:

> ...it is well known how intractable the analysis of any body of documents of this kind can be, so untidy is it, so variable and contradictory in its dogmas and doctrines, so capricious in what it preserves and what it must leave out. Most deceptive of all is the tendency of literary commentators and disputants to make confident assertions on subjects which they know little about, or which they could not in fact have known anything about, since the requisite information did not exist. To infer from such evidence what the whole content of the attitude to children was amongst the élite minority would itself be an uncertain task, still more so to make a reliable

decision on how far this attitude represents what all, or nearly all, persons experienced as children or acted upon as parents. And to attempt to go further and reconstruct on this basis the childhood experience and the childrearing practice of a whole society, from the kings and the queens and the nobles with their great bodies of advisors and servants, down to the farmers, craftsmen, peasants and labourers in their little houses, cottages and shacks, would be formidable indeed.

P. LASLETT, *Family Life and Illicit Love in Earlier Generations*, 1977, pp.8-9.

The formation of personality in the Western family, Laslett believes, can best be accounted for by reference to sociohistorical influences. Four separate but interdependent characteristics can be identified:

1. The shape and membership of the familial group, which has been confined essentially to nuclear family form.
2. The age of women on marriage and during their child-bearing period, both of which in the West have been comparatively late.
3. The age gap between the spouses: a high proportion of wives have been older than their husbands.
4. The presence of members of the household not belonging to the family. Servants were the largest single occupation group up to the 1900s. The majority of children were servants before marriage.

Neither de Mause nor Laslett examines the effects of the process of schooling on the family. However, both approaches throw interesting light on attempts to account for the changing concept of childhood.

FURTHER READING

For a general history of family life in English society, see P. Laslett, *The World We Have Lost*, 2nd edition, 1971, which contains a good bibliography. W. van der Eyken's *Education, the Child and Society. A Documentary History 1900-1973*, 1973, gives a range of extracts relating to views of childhood. A good insight into official attitudes towards adolescence can be gained from J. Springhall, *Youth, Empire and Society. British Youth Movements 1883-1940*, 1977.

QUESTIONS

1. How far does Ariès' thesis, based on iconographical material, bear out the fact that the family was not centrally concerned with child-rearing in the Middle Ages?
2. Examine the implications of research findings on adolescence for

curriculum planning.
3. What theories of childhood are represented in present day primary and secondary school practices?

7
Politics of the Curriculum
Denis Lawton

It is a mistake to assume that politics is concerned only with party politics. When the phrase 'politics and the curriculum' is used, the intention usually is to discuss who controls the curriculum, especially school curricula. This is a question which was ignored for a long time, but which has become fashionable in recent years. It has become topical for two reasons. First, because the sociologists of knowledge, or some of them, have suggested that the function of schooling is to control rather than to educate, and that the school curriculum is the major means of securing a docile and obedient working class. The second, and more plausible, explanation for the interest in the control of the curriculum, is that it is only in relatively recent years that any controversy has existed about the content of the curriculum. If there is no argument about what is in the curriculum, then there is unlikely to be any problem about who is controlling it. But when the curriculum becomes controversial, then it is likely that different pressure groups will form, each wanting to have some influence or control over the content of education.

There is a third reason for discussing the control of the curriculum. A useful definition of curriculum is 'a selection from the culture of a society'. This has the virtue of being uncontroversial (what else could a curriculum be?), but a serious question is begged. If we talk about the curriculum in terms of a selection from everything which is available in a society for possible transmission to the next generation, then the major question becomes 'who decides on what is selected?' The kind of selection which is made may have some connection with the social position of the decision makers, but that should not commit us to a naïve Marxist point of view which suggests that the curriculum selected will be either a reflection of 'bourgeois' values and knowledge because the decision makers are of that social category, or, that what is selected is a deliberately inferior kind of educational experience. The picture which will emerge for analysis is likely to be much more complicated than that; it is also probable that in a pluralist society control is likely to be dispersed rather than concentrated at one point.

Who selects? One easy answer is that teachers decide on the selection from the culture to produce a curriculum. This is only partly true. And it is more true for head teachers and heads of departments than for assistant teachers. But even then there are many constraints: HMI, local advisers, LEA administrators, governors, examining boards, parents, employers, etc., all of whom exert some kind of influence on what is taught and even how it is taught. It is also worth noting that some of these pressures are becoming stronger. As a result of a kind of consumerism in education, parents, for example, are becoming more vocal and this was expressed in the Taylor Report, 1977, on School Governing Bodies. At a more general level, the Tyndale scandal was important in establishing that there were limits to teachers' freedom in deciding on the curriculum. In this celebrated case, parents rebelled against the curriculum, or perhaps non-curriculum, which became the selection from the culture at William Tyndale Primary School and forced the LEA to take action. The head teacher and a number of assistant teachers were eventually dismissed.

Another version of the answer 'teachers decide the curriculum' is that there is a long tradition in England of complete freedom for teachers to plan their own curriculum. This is untrue: elementary schools were only given this freedom in 1926 and even after that they were following the guidelines published in *The Handbook of Suggestions for Teachers*, 1905 and revised in 1937; secondary schools were controlled by regulations until they were superseded by the 1944 Education Act. In addition, Bell and Grant (1974), in their discussion of this as one of the myths of education, pointed out that as far back as Queen Elizabeth I, the curricula of grammar schools were subject to a good deal of government interference.

It is true, however, that since 1944 teachers in this country have had a good deal more control over the curriculum than operates in almost every other society. The reasons for this are in themselves of political interest. Until 1833, there was no problem about state control of the curriculum because the government had adopted the policy of avoiding financial involvement, remaining content to leave the control of schools, and their curricula, to religious bodies. Attempts by Lord Brougham between 1816 and 1818 to involve the government in elementary education had failed because his proposals were too ambitious — involving a good deal of money and government interference which was contrary to the prevailing policy of *laissez-faire*. In 1833, Mr John Roebuck, a radical MP, asked the House of Commons to consider 'the means of establishing a system of national education' on the grounds that it would promote political tranquility and public virtue. But his scheme was also too ambitious and included state control of the curriculum which was rejected by the House of Commons. However, there was by now enough support for the idea of giving some help to the education of the lower orders that three weeks later Lord Althorp, Chancellor of the Exchequer, included a sum of £20,000 in the report of the Committee of Supply. This money was to be made available to the two religious societies (one Church of England, one non-conformist) to be spent on filling in the gaps of the existing provision of schools for the poor. By 1839, the amount of money needed had increased, and a committee of the Privy Council was sent up to superintend the spending of the money. Dr James Kay was appointed Secretary and he made the award of grants to schools conditional upon favourable report by HMI. But still the demand for money increased. In 1858, a commission was appointed under the chairmanship of the Duke of Newcastle to enquire into popular education. One of the recommendations of the *Newcastle Report*, 1861, was that more inspection was necessary. This recommendation was taken even further in the 1862 *Revised Code* which set out the conditions on which grants were to be paid, stating specifically the content of the elementary curriculum in terms of the 'three Rs'. Schools would receive a grant according to the number of pupils at various standards who reached the required degree of competency. This system of 'payment by results' was gradually modified but lasted in some form until the end of the nineteenth century.

1862 was probably the lowest point of teacher power. The history of the NUT and their view of professionalism can be seen as a reaction against the system of 'payment by results' (Tropp, 1959).

In 1926 the Regulations controlling the elementary curriculum were abolished. The reason for this 'act of liberation' is disputed (see John White, 1975), as is the disappearance of the Secondary Regulations after 1944. White suggests that the central authority's apparent liberalism in handing over control of the curriculum from the centre to the teaching profession was a fear of left-wing government rather than a demonstration of faith in the teaching profession.

The mid-40s to mid-1960s were the golden years of teacher control. The end of Secondary Regulations was strengthened by a reluctance by Labour ministers of education to interfere in curriculum matters. Also, in 1951 the five-subject group examination (School Certificate) was replaced by GCE 'O' levels which would be awarded for single subjects. But by 1960 there were signs of a changing attitude at the centre: the Conservative Minister of Education, Sir David Eccles, set up a Curriculum Study Group. This was opposed not only by teachers but also by local education authorities who were disturbed by this apparent bid by the central authority for curriculum control. The united opposition of teachers and LEAs was successful and the Curriculum Study Group was replaced in 1964 by the Schools Council for

Politics of the Curriculum

Curriculum and Examinations on which teachers were to have the majority in all important committees.

But the teaching profession did not make the most of its power to control the school curriculum. It failed to produce any kind of national policy, and even working through the Schools Council, the policy seemed to be a continuation of *laissez-faire*. One of the major criticisms of the Schools Council has been that its policy on curriculum has been to follow a kind of 'cafeteria approach'. In the 60s and 70s very little work was done on the curriculum as a whole, and those reports that were concerned with this subject were not of the highest quality.

This problem was made more acute by the fact that criticism about education and about teachers intensified through the 60s and early 70s. Progressive methods and curriculum innovation as well as comprehensive schools were subjects of frequent complaint. This was perhaps partly due to a general disillusionment about the possibility that education could solve our social and economic problems, but also connected with the rise of consumerism in education. As well as this, employers and others raised questions about falling standards. The DES set up the Assessment of Performance Unit in 1974. Two years later the new Permanent Secretary at the DES, James Hamilton, made public his view that teachers were too fond of sheltering behind their expertise when complaints were made by parents and employers. Ann Corbett, 1976, in the Fabian Society's evidence to the Taylor Committee, suggested that parents should be represented as of right on school governing bodies which should have greater control over the curriculum.

The years 1969 to 1979 represent a decade of declining teacher control of curriculum. At the end of that period, the revised constitution of the Schools Council symbolized this change when teachers lost their built-in majority vote on the Schools Council committees. The reasons for the decline of teacher control are complex, and some of them have already been touched upon above.

Maurice Kogan (1978), suggests that as early as 1960 there were signs that the consensus period in education was over. Many people, including politicians, were becoming disenchanted with education as the major method of improving society or solving social problems. The first *Black Paper*, 1969, was a symptom rather than a cause of this more questioning and critical attitude to education—especially 'progressive' education. The next reason for the decline of teacher control is concerned with wider participation in control of education as well as other institutions. The consumer movement in education as well as new versions of democracy and 'open government' gave rise to demands to participate in decision making, and, therefore to deny that teachers alone had a right to make decisions about curriculum in schools. Ann Corbett, for example,

Politics of the Curriculum

has suggested that the curriculum was too important to be left to the teachers.

Another reason was the accountability movement. Accountability is itself a difficult educational issue (see Chapter 8). One version of accountability would be closely allied to the question of participation; a cruder version simply demands 'value for money'. The 1976 Report of the House of Commons Expenditure Committee included both kinds of demand. The Prime Minister's Ruskin Speech in 1976 also emphasized another aspect of accountability when he demanded that education should be more concerned with the specific needs (especially manpower needs) of an industrial society.

A much publicized aspect of accountability in the 1970s was concerned with the suspicion that schools were less efficient than they should be, and that it was extremely difficult to call teachers to account when it was suspected that they were abusing their high degree of freedom. The most dramatic example of this was the William Tyndale Primary School scandal where some teachers appeared to be preaching politics as well as neglecting their traditional duties of teaching basic skills. Many complained about the lack of power by the local education authority to resolve this difficulty. Others suggested that it would always be extremely difficult for a local authority to take action on an inadequate curriculum unless much stronger guidelines were laid down nationally.

This kind of argument strengthened the hand of the DES in bidding for increased power over the curriculum. Prior to the Prime Minister's Ruskin speech in 1976, James Callaghan had reacted to criticisms about 'standards' by asking Fred Mulley, then Secretary of State for Education, to produce a report on schools. This 'secret' report (popularly referred to in the press as the Yellow Book) was leaked and became part of the background of the so-called Great Debate on Education. The DES appeared to have used the opportunity to discredit the Schools Council and its teacher control, and to take a more dynamic role itself. The first evidence of this new attitude by the DES was the *Green Paper* (1977). Here it was stated that the Secretaries of State could not abdicate from their responsibilities concerning the curriculum and the possibility of a core curriculum, or common curriculum was tentatively put forward. Much less tentative was the LEA Curriculum Review which was required by the DES. LEAs were asked to report on curricular arrangements and their plans for the future. When the results of this survey were published in November 1979 (*Local Authority Arrangements for the School Curriculum: Report on Circular 14/77 Review*) it was found that on many important issues, the majority of LEAs had no policy at all, or, what appeared to be inadequate planning.

This 'new-look' DES appeared to be reinforced by a revitalized

Inspectorate. In December 1977 HMI produced a 'discussion document', *Curriculum 11-16,* which strongly advocated a common curriculum. In 1979, the HMI Secondary Survey was published under the title *Aspects of Secondary Education in England*. This survey was in general supportive of teachers. But there were obvious areas of weakness. In particular, HMI suggested that option schemes and the 16 + examination structure encouraged a proliferation of subjects and a neglect of certain basic areas such as mathematics and science. Once again, the idea of a central curriculum appeared to be gathering strength.

After the 1944 Education Act the dominant metaphor regarding control of the curriculum was partnership. A triangle of power was envisaged with the central authority (DES), the local education authorities, and the teachers, each occupying one point on the triangle. There were many ambiguities associated with this metaphor: for example, partnership does not specify which partner has more or less control. Perhaps even more important than that was the idea of 'teachers' representing one side of the triangle. It has never been clear whether this means the teachers' unions or individual teachers, or teachers on such bodies as the Schools Council. By the end of the 1970s it began to look as though this partnership model had broken down and the prevailing metaphor now was 'accountability'. Two possibilities existed: either a centrally imposed national curriculum with teachers as mere functionaries; or, a central and agreed framework which would be professionally interpreted by teachers (meaning a professional body of teachers). For the second alternative to work, accountability would have to be spelt out. But as we shall see in the next chapter, accountability is an extremely difficult concept to define and even more difficult to apply to education. By 1980 these problems of the control of the curriculum were by no means resolved.

FURTHER READING

There are three short, very readable books which would serve to develop the arguments contained in this short chapter. *The Politics of Educational Change*, 1978, by Maurice Kogan is concerned with the whole field of education but Chapter 4 deals specifically with curriculum and students. The whole book should however be read. The *Politics of Curriculum Change* by Tony Becher and Stuart Maclure, 1978, is particularly useful for putting the English curriculum scene into an international context of change. *The Politics of the School Curriculum* by Denis Lawton, 1980, attempts to answer questions about the control of the curriculum by examining the role of the DES, the Schools Council, and APU and the examination system.

Politics of the Curriculum

QUESTIONS
1. To what extent is it true that the DES is seeking greater control over the curriculum?
2. Is it likely that the APU will have no effect on the curriculum?

8
Accountability
Denis Lawton

In the last chapter it was suggested that 'accountability' as a concept was being used increasingly frequently in discussions about the control of the curriculum. This chapter will attempt to clarify the meaning of accountability; to point out some of the dangers that have arisen when accountability models are developed (especially in the USA); and, finally, to suggest possible future developments in the UK.

Accountability, like many other second-hand concepts, is vague, ambiguous and of doubtful applicability in education. It is fairly easy to give reasons why a move towards accountability arose: the first is related to a concern for standards; the second more directly connected with economy.

Standards
At a time of educational change, parents worry about the level of their children's attainment; employers criticize the ability of school leavers. They want teachers to be accountable for the methods they are using, and for changes being made in the curriculum.

Financial Cuts
The second explanation for the rise of the accountability movement is more directly connected with money. Education systems have insatiable appetites for resources. No matter how much is spent on teachers, books, laboratory equipment, or school buildings, more is always needed. From time to time a halt is called, especially when money is scarce, and ratepayers, taxpayers, politicians and civil servants demand to know exactly what the money is being spent on, and an assessment of the benefits being purchased. They want to be reassured that they are getting value for money, or to have an excuse for reducing expenditure. They hold teachers responsible or accountable for the money being spent.

So far so good. Both reasons for accountability — if not carried too far — might be regarded as justifiable, or even common sense. Why not hold teachers accountable for the money spent on education in just the

Accountability

same way as company directors are accountable to shareholders? The directors may be the experts, but the shareholders have a right to know. Is this not analogous to teachers and parents?

That sounds sensible until the argument is pressed further. In the case of directors and shareholders the account rendering relationship is perfectly clear, but in education much less so. There are essentially two major problems: first, lack of clarity about the kind of account that has to be rendered; second, doubt about to whom the account should be rendered.

Whereas it is usually comparatively simple to look at an account of a profit-making company in order to examine how resources have been used and what has been gained as a result, it is much less easy in education. The results of a commercial company can be seen simply in terms of products and profits: x pounds invested; y motor cars produced and sold; z pounds profit. In education the amount of money invested can be calculated, but there the analogy finishes. Here, there is no equivalent.

Or is there? That is where the argument in recent years really begins. Some would like to assert that it should be possible to measure the product of education in terms of pupil learning achievements, and that we ought to be able to calculate 'profit' rather than simply assume that education, and more education, is automatically ' a good thing'. That view of education as one of investment and profit might be reinforced by the argument that we all know that some schools are better than others, so why not 'objectify' these good qualities as products (learning outcomes) that can be measured, and then relate this to the resources spent? The public has a right to know, it is argued. A crude version of that position exists when parents and others demand that an LEA produces a 'league table' of GCE examination results, so that 'good' schools can be identified and 'bad' schools castigated for their poor achievement/low profitability. More sophisticated versions exist (and will be discussed later in this chapter): it might also be argued that 16 + examinations present an incomplete picture of what a school produces, and also that examinations are notoriously unreliable; therefore, it is necessary to define more closely *exactly* what a school is trying to do and then to measure success in terms of test scores.

Again, this view has a common-sense attraction. Of course, teachers should known what they are trying to teach! So, define it carefully and measure the success as seen in pupils' performance. This common-sense approach was adopted and refined into a theoretical system by R. W. Tyler and his associates in the USA long before the term 'accountability' was used in education in the late 1960s.

In 1949, Tyler produced a very influential book *Basic Principles of*

Curriculum and Instruction, which sought to persuade teachers to think of every curriculum, indeed, every lesson, as having clear objectives. This has developed over the years into the 'behavioural objectives movement', particularly important in the history of education in the USA in the twentieth century.

The curriculum planning by behavioural objectives movement rests on a number of assumptions — some of them extremely dubious.

1. That any educational programme or activity can and should be stated as a list of unambiguous, pre-specified objectives.
2. That an objective must be stated as 'outcomes', i.e. pupil performance not teacher intention.
3. That all outcomes must be measurable.

According to this model it would no longer be satisfactory to have such aims as 'developing an understanding of scientific method; this general aim would be regarded as meaningless and would have to be operationalized into a series of precise pupil performances which could be pre-specified and later measured.

A number of education theorists have pointed out the objections to this kind of approach (for example, Stenhouse, 1975, Sockett, 1976).

The first objection is that education is essentially a long-term process, whereas the behavioural objectives approach deals in short-term pupil performance. Immediate results may be important and it may be useful to measure them, but education is essentially concerned with the delayed reactions and accumulated benefits. It is comparatively easy for history teachers, for example, to test whether pupils have remembered the events of a particular period in history studied that week or term: it is much more difficult to know whether that teaching-learning episode has any effect on attitudes and knowledge ten or 20 years later. But from an education point of view, the second is much more important. Even though teachers find it extremely difficult to measure their success in those terms they should, nevertheless, bear in mind that aim as well as the more limited immediate short-term results. The objectives approach, however, has the opposite effect, namely, emphasizing the short-term at the expense of the long-term.

That brings us to the second objection which is concerned with the difficulty of measuring learning success. Advocates of the behavioural objectives approach would have us believe that they can test any change brought about by learning. An opposing point of view is that it is much more difficult to measure learning successfully than the testers suggest, and much more difficult in the case of attitudes and values than in measuring simple skills and memorized information. Once again the danger is that the testers will concentrate on what they know they can test and this will inevitably distort what teachers teach.

A more fundamental objection is that the model of measuring output in terms of products is simply not appropriate for education. Stenhouse, 1975, for example, suggests that a process or input model is to be preferred. It is simply neither possible nor desirable to pre-specify all outcomes in the teaching-learning situation. This should be recognized and teachers should concentrate on being confident that the 'input' is worthwhile. To some extent an act of faith is always necessary about the results that good teaching will have. Although an English literature teacher might have a very clear view of the general direction that he would like a discussion of a poem to go, he cannot (and should not) be able to pre-specify the exact nature of pupils' responses to that poem.

The behavioural objectives approach claims to be 'scientific', but the view of knowledge built into the model is quite out of keeping with philosophy of science and philosophy of knowledge. Popper, 1963, for example, claims that the scientific approach is to make use of a hypothesis until it is refuted, but never to regard a hypothesis many times confirmed as 'the truth'. (The observation of one million white swans does not prove that all swans are white...) But the behavioural objectives view of knowledge is that of certainty: the teacher must know exactly what correct answer he wants from a pupil; he must know exactly what response he wants a pupil to give to a poem. By building up a collection of correct responses, the pupil becomes educated and this can be measured. This is both philosophically and educationally naïve.

There are also philosophical objections to the view of psychology which is built into the behavioural objectives approach. This view of curriculum assumes that behaviourist psychology is the only possible one. But Charles Taylor, 1964, and others have demonstrated the shortcomings of the behaviourist position. Hugh Sockett has applied these criticisms particularly to the educational use of behaviourism (Sockett, 1973). There are problems, for example, of what counts as behaviour. There are also familiar problems about the difficulty of regarding language as 'verbal behaviour'. More fundamentally, the anti-behaviourists argue that behaviourism tries to treat human beings as if they were machines rather than people. Certainly in education precisely those aspects of 'behaviour' not recognized by the behaviourists (for example, enjoying a poem or a symphony) are regarded as the high point of human experience even if they cannot be easily measured.

Accountability is not, of course, necessarily limited to an objectives view of curriculum, but the logic of the accountability metaphor leads us in that direction, as we shall see later when we examine the US experience.

Accountability

The second problem that I suggested earlier in connection with applying the accountability model to education was the difficulty of clarifying 'accountability to whom?' Sockett (1980) has suggested that arguments could be advanced on different grounds for a teacher's accountability to:

a) individual pupils and parents;
b) pupils and their parents as part of the community;
c) a teacher's employers e.g. the LEA;
d) the providers of the resources, both LEA and government;
e) the professional peers inside and outside the school;
f) other relevant educational institutions e.g. universities, secondary schools;
g) the public;
h) industry including the trade unions.

Sockett suggests that such a list is too slack and diffuse for us to be able to build a system of accountability from it. Yet we may have to try. Certainly the pattern of accountability here is much more complex than the company directors being responsible to a group of shareholders. But perhaps the analogy does not break down completely. The company directors are also responsible to other groups as well as the shareholders: income tax inspectors, various other government agencies, as well as their own work force. If the accountability model is to work in education, however, it will be necessary to specify the kind of account which has to be rendered to several different groups.

Recent US Experience of Accountability
Although the word 'accountability' has only been applied to education since the late 1960s (Lessinger, 1971), the history of applying business methods, values and terminology to education in the United States goes back much further. Callahan (1962) in a book aptly titled *Education and the Cult of Efficiency*, pointed out that the adoption of business values and practice in educational administration had started about 1900 and that by about 1930 'school administrators perceived themselves as business managers...school executives rather than as scholars and educational philosophers' (Preface). Callahan explains this by suggesting that American culture is dominated by the world of business; businessmen possess higher status and prestige than academics, so it was very likely that educational administrators would identify with the world of business rather than with the values of schools and universities. Callahan suggests that by 1907 there were indications that aspects of the business ideology had been accepted and were being applied by educators

themselves. He suggests that a key book was *Classroom Management* by William C. Bagley. Bagley saw school management as

> a problem of economy: it seeks to determine in what manner the working unit of the school plant may be made to return the largest dividend upon the material investment of time, energy and money. From this point of view, classroom management may be looked upon as a 'business' problem...
>
> R. E. CALLAHAN, *Education and the Cult of Efficiency*, 1962, p.7.

Another well-known administrator, J. F. Bobbitt, turned his attention in particular to the curriculum (see also Chapter 10). Bobbitt, who was a Professor in the University of Chicago, exerted a very great influence through the National Society for the Study of Education. One of his major contributions was *The Supervision of City Schools* (published as the Twelfth Yearbook of that Society in 1913). This was essentially a follow-up to an earlier study 'The Elimination of Waste in Education' published in the *Elementary School Journal* in 1912.

Bobbitt's major intention was to apply to schools the Taylor System of business efficiency and factory organization. For Bobbitt, efficiency in education meant the adoption of definite standards and the use of measurement scales which made it possible to report results in quantitative terms. Bobbitt admitted that under the system he was proposing education would require an even more elaborate system of accounting than a factory or a railroad, but he suggested that such records had been profitable in business and they were 'an indispensable basis for efficient management, direction and supervision' (Callahan, 1962, p.85).

Bobbitt saw his system simply in terms of applying 'science' or scientific method to education. His ideas and those of others advocating factory schools etc., were never totally accepted in the USA but their influence continued for a number of years. It is, for example, important historically to view the 'progressivism' of John Dewey partly as a reaction against this supposedly 'scientific' mentality in education.

A number of writers on accountability (Atkin, 1979 and House, 1975) have suggested that the time was ripe for a revival of these ideas in the 1950s and 1960s. When Lyndon Johnson became President of the USA he was apparently so impressed with Robert MacNamara, who had transferred from the Ford Motor Company to the Department of Defence and brought with him the managerial techniques of industry, that he ordered all government departments to adopt business efficiency methods. These included management by objectives, cost benefit analysis, systems analysis and planned programme budgeting. Seminars were held between 1965 and 1967 to encourage administrators in education to learn from the Department of Defense. Input and output models began to be applied to schools and welfare programmes.

This process of applying efficiency to education was undoubtedly assisted by the existence of the behavioural objectives school of curriculum planning. A justifying theory in education now existed which certainly looked more like an educational theory than the crude business efficiency views of Bobbitt and his colleagues 40 years earlier. Behavioural objectives became a major aspect of the accountability projects in the 1960s. Many educationists protested but they tended to be brushed aside in the name of progress and efficiency:

> Some voices were heard suggesting that schools strive for goals that went beyond those that could be stated readily in behavioural terms, and that behavioural objectives were undesirably limiting. However, the apparent logic of behaviourally stated objectives had tremendous appeal, not only to the general public when it heard about them, but to many teachers and school administrators.
>
> J. M. ATKIN, 1979, p.6.

Perhaps the best known example of accountability applied to education was the Michigan State Accountability System. The Michigan plan called for specially developed objective-referenced tests for all fourth and seventh graders in the state. A second stage of the plan involved the award of cash to schools on the basis of gains in achievement test scores. Test scores have also been made public, published in the newspapers, and compared with the scores in other schools.

The disadvantages of this system are similar to those of the nineteenth century 'payment by results' in England. The assumption was made that measuring a child's performance was a fair way of evaluating teaching skill or conscientiousness. The Michigan Education Association, representing about 80,000 teachers, was critical of the Michigan Plan. In 1973, the National Education Association (the largest teachers' union in the USA) became concerned that the plan might spread to other states. It therefore commissioned an independent evaluation which reported in 1974 (House, Rivers and Stufflebeam, 1974). This independent evaluation criticized the way the Michigan goals had been derived, the construction of the tests, the lack of participation by teachers, and a number of other technical points. The Michigan administrators replied and the controversy continued for many years. It is not necessary for us to enter into that particular debate, but it is clear that test programmes of

Accountability

that kind encourage a narrowing of the curriculum and teaching style which is over-didactic. Teachers concentrate on those items which they think will come up in a test rather than on what they believe to be most worthwhile. There are also very heavy administrative burdens based on teachers giving out, marking and checking tests, thus leaving them less time to do more imaginative teaching. A fuller discussion of the debate about accountability in the USA can be found in *School Evaluation: The Politics and the Process* by E. R. House, 1973.

The Future of Accountability in the UK
So we can decide either to reject the accountability model altogether, or to recognize its limitations and make sure that any version applied to education is appropriate. If we reject the model completely two further problems arise. First, the decision-makers may not accept the rejection and may impose a system of accountability on education which would distort the educational process. Second, we would still have to find a means of satisfying legitimate demands from various groups for information about what is going on within the educational system. It may, therefore, be preferable to accept accountability, but to make sure that the model is adapted sufficiently to education to ensure that the worst excesses of the model are avoided and that the teaching-learning processes within the schools are not distorted.

Accountability is, as we have seen, very close to evaluation. Barry MacDonald (see Ch. 15 of this book) has suggested three ideal type styles of evaluation which he calls autocratic, bureaucratic and democratic. MacDonald's preferred style, democratic evaluation, is concerned with providing information for the whole community. I would like to attempt to outline a system of democratic accountability which would bear in mind the problem raised by Sockett about the difficulty of knowing 'accountable to whom'. This problem is made even more complicated by the fact that it would seem to me that the discussion about accountability so far has been concerned with one-way 'upward accountability', that is, a subordinate giving an account to a superior for money spent, resources used etc. But democratic accountability should be a two-way process: the teacher is accountable to pupils as well as to the headteacher or the inspector; the headteacher is accountable to his assistant teachers as well as to governors or the LEA. This may be shown diagrammatically as follows:

Whereas in bureaucratic accountability the process is linear and one-way (Figure 1)

Accountability

**Figure 1
Bureaucratic Accountability**

DES ← LEA ← Head Teacher ← Teacher ← Pupils

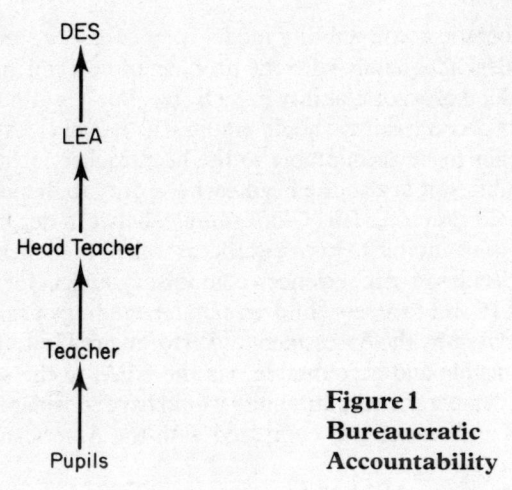

with democratic accountability the pattern is much more complex and is essentially a two-way process (Figure 2).

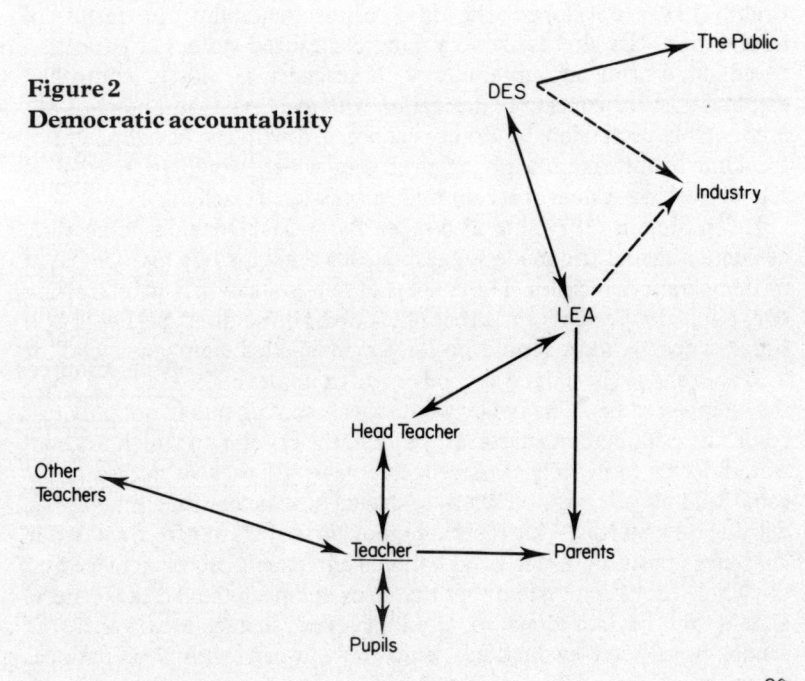

**Figure 2
Democratic accountability**

Accountability

The democratic accountability model is, of course, a simplification and does not deal adequately with the problem of how much accountability and what kind of accountability in each case. But it is important that such a system of accountability should emphasize that whereas it is reasonable for a teacher to be accountable to the headteacher for his professional responsibilities, it is also the headteacher's duty to demonstrate that he has allocated resources fairly, for example, between departments. He is, therefore, accountable to his assistants as well as to the LEA. Similarly if the DES decides to make science a compulsory subject for all pupils up to the age of 16 and to assess children's understanding of science by means of tests devised by the Assessment of Performance Unit, then the DES is also responsible and accountable, via the LEA, to the schools. Such a system of democratic accountability would have considerable advantages to schools and teachers as compared with the American models so far discussed.

We must also deal with the question of what kind of account should be rendered. Clearly, the kind of accountability based solely on test results, especially behavioural objectives tests, presents an inadequate picture of the educational programme of a school. Various attempts are being made, both in the UK and the USA, to develop evaluation and accountability strategies which will do more justice to the school's intentions. Michael Eraut (1979) developed the idea of accountability in terms of information. His alternative to a more centralized system of education based on central accountability with teachers as closely controlled employees, is the concept of delegation with teachers as autonomous but accountable professionals. Eraut is concerned with the development of the kind of information giving processes which would be needed at school level in a system of accountable professional teachers.

Helen Simons (1977) has also taken Barry MacDonald's democratic evaluation model and made suggestions for school *self-evaluation* based on democratic principles. The concept of self-evaluation is an interesting one, but it also presents a number of unsolved difficulties. Becher (1979) suggests that schools should no longer be labelled simply as 'good' or 'bad', but should be judged as good or bad examples of the kind of schools they happen to be. This policy would mean making public not only test results or examination successes, but also the criteria on which a school would decide to be judged. Arrangements would then be necessary for some kind of 'peer group review' to decide how successful a school was, within its own terms. This is perhaps moving too far away from a possible consensus position. Clearly, no national agreement can be achieved on the whole education system, but that does not mean that certain criteria should not be laid down. I would suggest that such a system of school-based self-evaluation could only work within a national framework. The democratic accountability in Figure 2 would have to be defined closely in such cases.

John Elliott (1979, 1980) has also written a number of papers concerned with 'self-accounting' schools. He is currently directing a research project exploring with a few secondary schools the problems they face in trying to develop their own accountability procedures (the Cambridge Accountability Project). Elliott feels that schools might be allowed to write their own accounts or reports which would then be checked by external auditors prior to release for publication. Here again, such a system would be more credible if there were some agreement nationally on a common curriculum. It would seem reasonable to suggest that schools should be accountable to LEAs and the DES for the structure of their curriculum, in order to ensure that unacceptable diversity was not taking place, but that having met those criteria, then the schools could be given much greater freedom to demonstrate their qualities, both within that agreed curriculum and beyond it. It would seem to be extremely likely that during the next few years some progress will be made in the direction of a nationally agreed common curriculum.

A more controversial development is that of the Assessment of Performance Unit which although not planned as a national accountability system, occasionally appears to be moving in that direction.

The intention to set up the APU was announced in August 1974. Originally it was intended as, or was stated to be, a means of testing the particular needs of the disadvantaged. It has rapidly become, however, a system of monitoring standards in schools. The intention is to monitor children's developments by means of at least six kinds of tests. The tests will be concerned with the following kinds of development: verbal, mathematical, scientific, ethical, (later called 'social and personal'), aesthetic, physical (modern languages and technological have also been suggested as other possible areas.)

APU officers (mostly HMI on secondment) have been careful to say that they want to minimize the 'backwash' effect of monitoring on the curriculum. But any official test inevitably encourages 'teaching to the test' and the APU will not be able to avoid this completely.

APU publications also emphasize that when reports on performance are published it will not be possible to identify individual pupils, schools or even LEAs. It is also important that the decision was made at an early stage that 'blanket testing' would not be used, but only 'light samples' of pupils in local education authorities. Perhaps the major objection to the APU is that at a time of financial stringency and cuts in other areas of education, this very expensive monitoring programme is being given priority. Others would argue that if testing is to go on then tests ought to

Accountability

be of a diagnostic kind to help schools rather than simply to monitor standards. This point is reinforced by technical arguments about item banking and the use of the Rasch Model (see Goldstein and Blinkhorn, 1977).

A greater problem may arise from the fact that the APU exercise will serve to legitimize local authority practices of a much more dubious nature. There are already signs that LEAs are developing their own batteries of tests which will not be subject to the same restrictions as those of the APU. In other words, 'blanket testing' may become the order of the day, and the results of these tests could easily be made available. This would then begin to have some of the features of the American accountability exercises already described.

Clearly, there is a need for the public in general, and parents in particular, to be informed of what is happening in our schools, including certain information about standards. It is also important that certain national rules apply so that cases such as William Tyndale should not recur. On the other hand, it is to be hoped that we will not over-react and find ourselves in the position of over-testing, and, worse still, a curriculum planned by objectives. A middle way is possible: namely, a democratic view of accountability, and a view of 'accounting' which does not rest too heavily on performance on tests. Both of these aspects, however, need a good deal more work.

FURTHER READING

William Bacon's *Public Accountability and the Schooling System,* 1978, is useful for the nineteenth-century background (Chapter 1) as well as a sociological analysis of one LEA. Ernest House's *School Evaluation,* 1973, discusses the American experience from a wide range of theoretical and practical perspectives. Sockett (1980) explores the philosophical problems.

QUESTIONS
1. Why is it suggested that 'accountability', which works well as a concept in commerce, cannot be directly applied to education?
2. What problems are likely to arise from self-accounting in schools?

9
Management and Participation in Curriculum Decision-Making

Peter Gordon

Schools and Teachers

We have already seen in the last chapter that in recent years there has been a shift from the traditional view that, based on his or her professional judgement, the teacher should be autonomous in making curriculum decisions, to a position where the claims of other interested parties need to be considered.

This message was clearly spelt out in the so-called Green Paper, *Education in Schools. A Consultative Document,* 1977. The section headed 'Curriculum' pin-points some of the weaknesses in the existing arrangement. In the primary schools, the child-centred approach

> has proved to be a trap for some less able or less experienced teachers who applied the freer methods uncritically or failed to recognize that they require careful planning of the opportunities offered to children and systematic monitoring of the progress of individuals. (p.8)

Middle schools, with their small staffs, find difficulty in offering the range of specialisms required. Since comprehensive education has become the accepted mode of secondary schooling, the curriculum has been under great pressure from constantly growing demands upon it. New content and new styles of learning, a wider spectrum of students' abilities and an overloaded curriculum have not been matched by a supply of appropriately qualified and experienced teachers.

Four major concerns are expressed in the document:

1. the curriculum differs from school to school and therefore gives rise to inequality of opportunities for pupils;
2. with a mobile population, there needs to be a standard minimum similarity of curriculum across the country;

3. priorities within the curriculum have not been established by schools. Choice therefore becomes more difficult for pupils;
4. the curriculum is not sufficiently matched to life in a modern society.

For these reasons, the Green Paper suggested that there should be a 'protected' or 'core' element of the curriculum common to all schools. It would not necessarily be uniform, but it would 'offer reassurances to employers, parents and the teachers themselves'. (p.11)

One of the major difficulties in carrying out changes as suggested above is the lack of any apparent framework within schools for participating in curricular decision-making and for effectively carrying it out. (Unlike further and higher education, schools do not have Academic Boards.) The Green Paper does not explore the attempts which have been made within schools to make this possible such as the creation of faculty structures and members of staff with named curriculum responsibilities. Obviously, much depends on the size of the school, but practices vary. Some suggestions have been made in the HMI document *Curriculum 11-16* for structural patterns which will facilitate curriculum decision-making. It recognizes the academic-pastoral dimensions of a school and the existing hierarchy of status, as reflected in scale posts, which act as inhibiting factors in change. At present too, younger and inexperienced teachers are often unable effectively to express their views.

The document sets out five different models, which have a number of features common to them all. It assumes that:

1. one deputy head will be concerned with curriculum and not, as is customary, be responsible for either pupils or staff;
2. subjects and deparments have been replaced at senior levels by posts which require the holders to note what is happening across the whole curriculum;
3. instead of heads of department being responsible for curricular ideas and the money to implement them, a new senior post would be created, the occupant to be responsible for resources and finances.

An example will indicate how the new structure would operate. Based on a school of 900 pupils, the organization might be as follows:

Management and Participation in Curriculum Decision-Making

Use of structure

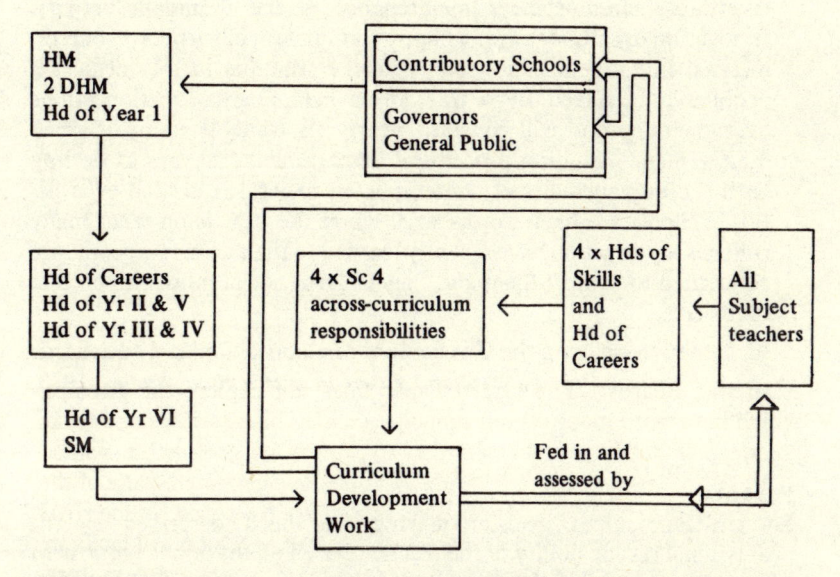

```
┌─────────────┐      ┌──────────────────────┐
│ HM          │◄─────│ Contributory Schools │◄──┐
│ 2 DHM       │      ├──────────────────────┤   │
│ Hd of Year 1│      │ Governors            │◄──┤
└──────┬──────┘      │ General Public       │   │
       │             └──────────────────────┘   │
       ▼                                        │
┌──────────────┐  ┌─────────────┐  ┌─────────┐  │  ┌──────────┐
│ Hd of Careers│  │ 4 x Sc 4    │  │ 4 x Hds │  │  │ All      │
│ Hd of Yr II&V│  │ across-     │◄─│ of Skills│◄─┼──│ Subject  │
│ Hd of Yr III │  │ curriculum  │  │ and     │  │  │ teachers │
│ & IV         │  │ responsibil.│  │ Hd of   │  │  │          │
└──────┬───────┘  └──────┬──────┘  │ Careers │  │  └──────────┘
       │                 │         └─────────┘  │       ▲
┌──────┴──────┐          ▼                      │       │
│ Hd of Yr VI │   ┌─────────────┐   Fed in and  │       │
│ SM          │──►│ Curriculum  │───assessed by─┴───────┘
└─────────────┘   │ Development │
                  │ Work        │
                  └─────────────┘
```

The structure is to be used to ensure that any curriculum development has been considered by those teachers who have cross-curriculum responsibilities. Information about development of work is also fed automatically to the contributory schools, but their comments and reactions reach the school by a different route. Their comments, and others arising from outside, are separately considered by three groups, each with a slightly different function, to provide a view as to general practicability and desirability for staff and pupils, a view as to the impact on current practice and job opportunities, and a view on the output question, closely linked with the resource and financial implications. Only those who teach it are involved in monitoring the work.

Curriculum 11-16, 1977 p.77.

Whilst the document acknowledges the possible effects of declining roles in such planning, their implications for management and decision-making are not made clear. The older the age of the pupil the more staff-intensive are the options offered and therefore expensive to operate. Redeployment of teachers within as well as between schools can also present difficult problems: this can result in a mismatch between the desirable curriculum and the staff available to teach it. One writer has summed up the two forces at work in practical curriculum planning at the present time, those of maintenance and innovation.

> Maintenance is the task of delivering the services of schooling effectively to the mass of pupils; innovation is the task of keeping up

with the times, modernizing and revitalizing the teaching. Even in favourable circumstances maintenance is the dominant activity. Innovation usually waits for a happy conjunction of surplus resources, internal initiative and a strong external stimulus in the form of a problem to be solved. In contraction the maintenance function will be overwhelming and will consume nearly all available energy. Skilled management including procedural management (the arts of dealing with the bureaucracies of contemporary society) is needed even for this. Schools are likely to discover when the heat is on what many colleges of education have recently learned to their cost: few people are concerned to protect them and they lack the social muscle to protect themselves.

K. SHAW, 'Managing the Curriculum in Contraction' in C. Richards (ed.), *Power and the Curriculum: Issues in Curriculum Studies*, 1978, p.46.

Parents
So far, curriculum decision-making has been described as the professional responsibility of the teacher, based on his or her judgement and understanding of the perceived needs of students. The Plowden Report, *Children and their Primary Schools* (1967) drew attention to the association between parental encouragement and education performance (Vol. 1, Ch. 4, p.37). Studies indicate that there is often a gap between how teachers see their role in schools and how parents regard it. Although parents are represented on national bodies such as Schools Council, there is a less clearly defined direct relationship between teachers and parents. Parents may be unhappy with some aspects of a school's curriculum but feel powerless to make their views known. See for example, Schools Council *Enquiry 1 Young School Leavers*, 1968, pp.110-12. The situation has been expressed strongly by one teacher:

> There are often cases of enormous arrogance on the part of a head and his/her staff in relating with parents. We are undeniably accountable to each parent who — either through choice or not — entrusts his child to us for the duration of the child's formal education. We *must* make clear our aims, our values and our priorities: inform parents about the thinking behind changes of curriculum and organization and *expect* to be challenged by them as we work. We are, after all, working with *their* children. Parents often do not recieve the respect due them by schools; schools are often trapped by knowing that the necessary innovations are difficult for parents to appreciate, as they are quite outside their own former experience of school.

A. ELLIS, 'Institutional Autonomy and Public Accountability — A Response', in *Proceedings of the British Educational Administration Society*, Winter, 1975, p.30.

Local Authorities
At local authority level there are two aspects of decision-making which affect schools. The elected political representatives obviously influence both curriculum and management aspects. For example, at Tameside, Greater Manchester, it was possible, following a local election and a subsequent change of party in power, to reverse a previous decision and reinstate grammar schools. The other aspect is the professional element, consisting of the Chief Education Officer and his staff, who carry out the policies of the elected representatives.

At the management level, there have been difficulties in some authorities which have introduced corporate management systems. In an attempt to make education responsible to the whole authority rather than to a single committee, corporate managers have been appointed. This has lessened the powers of Education Officers and led to a blurring of the lines of decision-making; at Avon this resulted in the resignation of the Chief Education Officer as a protest. It is clear from the responses of local authorities to Circular 14/77 on arrangements made for the school curriculum that few authorities produce detailed policy statements ((1979), p.20, para. 2).

Local advisers may play a key role in initiating (or discouraging) curriculum innovation, acting as a liaison between the school and the authority, recommending expenditure on resources in the form of equipment or extra teachers. Equally, where local testing has been instigated, this may have a dampening effect on innovation. Little information is available on the ways in which advisers operate, but a recent survey by Bolam reveals some interesting information. Out of 235 respondents from a sample of advisers in English LEAs which experienced minimal or no local government reorganization, 70 per cent had specialist subject responsibilities and the same percentage were involved in implementing curriculum projects. Most advisers saw themselves as facilitators of innovation but about one in three felt constrained from carrying out this role. Contacts with research and curriculum agencies, including the Schools Council, were relatively infrequent and advisers did not see themselves as being concerned with informing the schools of the work of such bodies or feeding back the results to the external agencies. This apparent reluctance to become involved in the process may stem from the fact that 82 per cent of the respondents had received no specific training for advisory work. (R. Bolam, G. Smith and H. Canter, 'Local Education Authority Advisers and Educational Innovation', in *Education Administration,* Vol. 6, No. 1, Winter, 1977/8, pp.28-9.)

There has also been a decline in the number of inspectors employed by local authorities in the last four years and this is reflected in the ratio of advisers to different subject areas. For example only half of the Outer London Boroughs have advisers for mathematics and English. Less than a third of all the authorities have specialist advisers for English, mathematics, science, history, geography, languages, art and craft, religious education, physical education and home economics. (See *Times Educational Supplement,* November 3, 1978.)

Examining Bodies
One of the main criticisms of examining bodies advanced by secondary school teachers is that curriculum decision-making is pre-empted by the demands made by examination syllabuses which are externally determined. It is true to say, however, that there have been developments in recent years which make this argument less convincing.

For one thing, since the Schools Council for the Curriculum and Examinations was established in 1964, 'new' subjects proposed for inclusion at examination level are discussed and subsequently monitored in detail by the relevant Subject Committees, which all have built-in teacher majorities. Such new proposals may come from subject associations speaking on behalf of member interests. These points remind us that when we are defining the role of the teacher in the process of curriculum decision-making it is important to identify the forum in which this is taking place. A teacher, for example, may be more powerful in effecting change outside the confines of his or her particular school.

It might be argued too, that the external control over examinations has been lessened by the introduction of the Certificate of Secondary Education (CSE) in 1964. The possibility of school-based Mode 3 examinations allowed for curriculum development: teachers became more active in examining boards and in evaluating the work of their own pupils. Opinions differ among teachers as to the merits of internally or externally set examinations. In a number of cases, Schools Council projects have discovered that by providing examinations linked to their programmes, this acts as an inducement to schools to adopt the projects. Examining boards are often accused of dictating to teachers what should be taught, thus gearing the curriculum to examination requirements, and of failing to respond fairly rapidly to contemporary developments.

The view has also been advanced by two experienced examiners, Macintosh and Smith (1975), that teachers are somewhat shy in taking the initiative in communicating their wishes to examining boards. There are several curriculum areas in school which do not correspond neatly to subjects; such obvious examples are inter-disciplinary studies and integrated work. At the same time, examining bodies tend to operate on a basis of assessing discrete subjects. In order to effect change, then, there is a need for a reassessment of the roles of both teachers and examining boards both in the ways in which they operate and more fundamentally, in the way in which they are organized.

The same writers make the suggestion that a group of teachers within a school involved in preparing an integrated studies programme should first map out the desired contents, attitudes and concepts within chosen subjects and then communicate the aims of the programme and the lists of subjects to examining boards. The latter, for their part, would, in considering the statement of aims, look into the assessment aspect of such programmes and prepare appropriate advisory services. Teachers might profitably be put in touch with teams in other schools undertaking similar work. Examining boards themselves might change their role, acting as closer partners with schools, provided enough school staff skilled and interested in examining on a continuous basis are available. This would facilitate both curriculum development and assessment practice (pp.124-5).

The introduction of a common system of examining at 16+ will go some way to meeting these suggestions. The document setting out the scheme mentions the 'unprecedented opportunity to review the nature and content of the curriculum as well as developing appropriate methods of assessment'. *(Examinations at 16+: Proposals For The Future*, 1975, p.65.) Much will depend on how far a largely teacher-controlled examination is matched by a knowledge of assessment procedures and an understanding of the bases of curriculum planning.

Central Government
The formal position in Britain on decision-making in curriculum matters in schools is not clear. Section 1 of the 1944 Education Act lays upon the Secretary of State for Education the duty to 'promote the education of the people and secure the effective execution by local authorities, under his control and direction of the national policy'. However, an Administrative Memorandum issued in 1945 stated that local education authorities 'shall determine the general education character of the school...Subject thereto, the governors shall have the general direction of the conduct and curriculum of the school'. There is a warning in Section 67 of the 1944 Act that the Secretary of State would, as a last resort, uphold the LEAs' right to impose its authority on governors and heads of schools in curriculum matters. In actual practice, the DES rarely interferes with LEA decisions of this sort; on the other hand, there is little or no evidence that governors normally play a direct part in

curriculum affairs. Their function is seen as one of general oversight of the school. In a large-scale survey of attitudes of governors, heads and local authorities conducted by Baron and Howell (1974), heads claimed that they were entirely responsible for deciding what was to be taught, reporting major changes to governors as matters of information: most governors said 'that they would never dream of interfering with the curriculum'. This state of affairs springs from the traditional view that the content of education should be left to the teachers and that laymen are not competent to challenge the head on curriculum matters (p.125)

The other aspect of governmental interest in the curriculum is represented by the activities of Her Majesty's Inspectors (HMI). Although still 'the eyes and ears of the Department' the Inspectors' role has been changing considerably during recent years (see, for example, 'Power Without Responsibility?' *The Times Educational Supplement*, 12 November, 1976). Whereas formerly individual schools were inspected and assessed, more emphasis is now placed on National Surveys, promoting curriculum discussion documents and providing in-service training and liaison work with a wide range of educational bodies. The number of Inspectors is decreasing. There were 411 at the beginning of 1977 — of these 100 are centrally based so that a swift response to urgent questions can be given, see Department of Education and Science *Annual Report for 1976*. (1977). The Inspectorate also acts as a link between central government and local education authorities, advising on curriculum matters where requested. Their direct impact on the decision-making process in schools is therefore difficult to assess.

Who should take the decisions?
This dispersal of powers of decision-making can be seen in a dramatic form in the recent case of the William Tyndale School. Here, in their own words: 'The teachers decided the children should be given as much choice and responsibility as the limitations of a school will allow. They were encouraged to consider the school as their building, could come in before school, stay afterwards, and have the choice of going out or staying in at play times. Common teacher/children areas were set up for use at these times.' (T. Ellis, B. Haddow, J. McWhirter and D. McColgan, *William Tyndale: The Teachers' Story*, 1976, p.68.) The staff consciously put all their efforts into helping the disadvantaged children: in doing so, they roused the opposition of parents, managers and the feeder infant school. The ILEA called on its Inspectorate to investigate whilst the DES remained on the sidelines. No firm conclusion could be drawn from the inspection, as there was no basis on which one school could be compared with another. (See J. Gretton, and M. Jackson, *William Tyndale: Collapse of a School — or a System?*, 1976, pp.85-96).

An inquiry headed by Robin Auld, QC began in October 1975 'into the teaching, organization and management' of the Tyndale School. It clearly emerged, during the course of the hearing, that the lines of communication and authority in decision-making were blurred. The Report mentioned the 'ill defined shared responsibility for the conduct and curriculum of the school' (para. 837) and also asked

> If the head teacher persists in ignoring the Inspector's strong advice, upon what basis can and should the Authority intervene? ...Is the head teacher to be left to go his own way until the Authority is satisfied that it is not fulfilling in the case of that school its fundamental statutory obligations and/or until there is sufficient evidence to justify disciplinary proceedings for inefficiency or misconduct? By that time the school may have deteriorated beyond recall.
>
> ILEA, *William Tyndale Junior and Infant School Public Inquiry*, 1976, para. 830.

Taylor Report and after

Whilst the Tyndale affair was being discussed, a Committee of Enquiry was appointed by the Secretary of State, headed by Mr Tom Taylor 'to review the arrangements for the management and government of maintaining primary and secondary schools in England and Wales, including the composition and functions of bodies of managers and governors'. (Department of Education and Science, *A New Partnership for our Schools*, 1977). At the beginning of Chapter 6, the Committee admitted that responsibility for the school curriculum was described by many witnesses as 'the most difficult, sensitive and controversial of the issues we had to consider.' (para. 6.4).

The Committee contested the claim that curriculum should be regarded as a preserve of a school's teachers (6.12). A wider cross-section of local opinion was required on governing bodies and this could be achieved by identifying four elements — the school staff, parents, local education authorities and the local community: each, it was suggested, should have equal representation (see Annexe to Ch. 4, p.35). The governing body would set the aims of the school for which they were responsible and these should be appraised by the local education authority. The starting point might be for the head and his colleagues to submit a first draft of the school's aims for the governing body's consideration. The latter would then consider 'whether the organization, teaching methods, disciplinary practices and other measures used in the school are appropriate for the pursuit of their aims.' (para. 6.26).

As a practical help, the Taylor Committee set out in an Appendix six examples of how suggestions for change might originate from a variety of interested parties. One of the examples concerns parental initiative in curriculum matters:

Consideration of a proposal to introduce the teaching of French into a primary school (ages 7-11)

1. Originator
A parent, in a letter to the headteacher.

2. Action by headteacher
  i. To acknowledge the proposal.
  ii. To hold preliminary consultations with the teaching staff.
  iii. To report to the next meeting of the governing body.

3. Action by governing body
Request to head, after further discussion with teachers, to consult local education authority adviser(s) and the appropriate secondary school(s) and to make full report on:
  i. the educational merits of the proposal;
  ii. the implications for the overall aims and objectives of the school;
  iii. the resource implications (teachers, books, equipment etc.);
  iv. effects on existing timetable, including the steps by which the teaching of French might be introduced;
  v. the steps necessary to monitor progress and evaluate the scheme if it is introduced, including any resource implications of such measures:
  vi. implications for other primary schools feeding the same secondary school(s).

Again, the division of action between 2 and 3 above is made simply for the purposes of this example: some heads would probably have taken some at least of the steps in 3 before bringing the matter before the governing body.

The governing body might decide to convene a meeting with representatives of the local education authority and the appropriate secondary school(s) to discuss the proposal further. This is clearly not a matter which the governing body should decide in isolation. Only the local education authority can decide whether additional resources can be provided. If the school were to attempt to proceed without additional resources (eg of staff, of equipment) its ability to achieve its agreed aims and objectives might be impaired.

The governing body would reach a decision in the light of all the considerations mentioned. If they decided to go ahead, they would ask the headteacher to take the necessary steps and to propose arrangements for monitoring the effects and effectiveness of the teaching so that it could be evaluated in due course. If they decided not go ahead, they would ask the head to convey and explain the decision to the parent. The matter would in due course be mentioned in the head's annual report.

DES, *A New Partnership For Our Schools,* 1977, p.217.

The response to these recommendations has naturally varied. The National Union of Teachers' commentary on the Taylor Report, entitled *Partnership in Education,* May, 1978, stated that the powers given to governors were too sweeping and 'inimical to the interests of children, parents and society generally' (4.6). Further, the education of children should be protected from the intrusion of non-professionals (4.7). The role of governors in respect of teaching methods, timetables and discipline was also stated to be 'unworkable'. (For a comment on the NUT response see P. Newell, 'Sheep, goats and governors,' in *The Times Educational Supplement,* 7 July, 1978.)

The Taylor Report brought to the fore the major difficulties facing any reform of curriculum decision-making. Some of these concerns have been voiced by Humble (1978). Can the governing bodies create partnership from potential conflict? Structural reform depends on people and processes: further attention to leadership styles and the decision-making processes is needed. Can governing bodies cope with the effects of zero growth in resource terms? Is there a discernible relationship between 'better education' and structural change? There are also other pressures leading to decision-making being taken elsewhere, not least in the political field, and the move towards local decision-making may have no real substance. And how far are local education authorities prepared to surrender some of their financial powers? (S. Humble, 'Governing Schools: Has the Taylor Report Got the Balance Right?' in *Education Administration,* Vol. 6, No. 1, Winter 1977/8, pp.17-18.) These questions remain to be answered.

FURTHER READING
H. L. Gray, *Change and Management in Schools,* especially Ch. 4, looks at some of the issues raised in this chapter. The role of advisers is further explored in R. Bolam, G. Smith and H. Canter, *LEA Advisers and the Mechanisms of Innovation,* 1978. Some of the essays contained in C. Richards (ed.), *Power and the Curriculum. Issues in Curriculum Studies,* 1978, especially Sections I to III are recommended.

Management and Participation in Curriculum Decision-Making

QUESTIONS
1. How can schools be organized in order to improve the process of decision-making?
2. What clashes of interest might arise under a more democratic form of decision-making on the curriculum?

PART THREE
CURRICULUM PLANNING

10
Models of Planning
Denis Lawton

Curriculum planning is a new subject in some ways but not in others. Plato was interested in what should and should not be taught, and to whom various subjects should be taught. (Incidentally, his view of different kinds of curriculum for different kinds of pupils—gold, silver, and base metals—is by no means dead.) But curriculum studies as a subject to be taken seriously even at university level is a comparatively new phenomenon. Curriculum is likely to be controversial at times of rapid social change. When teachers are doing what everyone expects of them, at no extra cost, and in the ways that teachers have traditionally carried out their duties, there is likely to be little discussion of the content of education or the curriculum. Curriculum studies and curriculum planning tend to emerge either when someone wants to change what is taught (or who is taught) or when educational costs are increasing, and politicians or others want to make sure that education does not cost too much, or that value for money can be assured.

So curriculum studies can be strongly associated either with social and educational change, or with movements towards accountability. And sometimes with both at the same time.

The different social events behind curriculum change will tend to give rise to different curriculum models. For example, perhaps the best known curriculum model is the objectives model (see below). Curriculum thinking is still much influenced today by two historical episodes which, long after the event, might be classified as examples of the objectives model. First, the rapid expansion of elementary education in England from 1834 to 1860, which gave rise to the objectives based *Revised Code* of 1862 and the system of primitive accountability known ever since as 'payment by results'. (See P. Gordon and D. Lawton, *Curriculum Change in the Nineteenth and Twentieth Centuries, 1978.*) Second, the rapid expansion of secondary education in the United States from 1890 onwards (see Kliebard, 1979) which gave rise to various attempts to apply factory 'efficiency' to schools, and in the writings of Franklin Bobbitt (1912 and 1918) to one of the first examples of a book in the field of curriculum studies.

Models of Planning

I want to suggest that there are, in fact, only three possible curriculum models. The first, I have already referred to as the objectives model; this is also called the factory model, or the output, or the product model. The second is referred to as the input model, or process model. The third, has been described as the situational analysis or cultural analysis model of curriculum. It may be worthwhile spending a little time on each of those three models.

1. The Curriculum Objectives Model

Kliebard, 1979, shows how the rapid expansion of secondary school education in the USA beginning in the 1890s led the National Education Association to appoint a series of committees. The reports of these committees were controversial and hence the story of curriculum studies in the USA began. Some of the controversy concerned the relation between high schools and admission to colleges. One of the most bitter arguments concerned Latin and Greek in the curriculum. The problem of the school curriculum being dominated by the needs, or supposed needs, of higher education has, of course, lasted a long time and in many other countries as well as the USA.

There is no need for us to go into all the details of the controversy and even conflict over the school curriculum in the USA at the turn of the century, but it is interesting that one very positive outcome was the growth of 'scientific curriculum making'. Bobbitt was a leading exponent of this 'rational' point of view. It is perhaps no coincidence that the title of one of his early contributions to the debate was 'The elimination of waste in education', *Elementary School Teacher*, Volume 12, No. 6, February, 1912. Kliebard shows how Bobbitt drew extensively from the work of F. W. Taylor, sometimes known as the father of the scientific management movement. In Taylor's major work *Principles of Scientific Management* he set out guidelines for an approach to industrial management by means of 'time and motion studies' which have had doubtful long-term results in industry. Nevertheless, Bobbitt devoted himself to translating the Taylor procedures into the field of curriculum making. Curriculum development thus became an attempt to standardize the means by which pre-determined specific outcomes could be achieved. Success should be judged by the extent to which the actual outcomes matched the predictions. It is for this reason that the behavioural objectives model is sometimes referred to as the factory model or the production model.

This objectives approach has stood the test of time in the USA, despite frequent and powerful attacks on the model. Perhaps the best known name is that of Ralph Tyler whose book *Basic Principles of Curriculum and Instruction,* 1949, continues to be of very great influence. The Tyler

Models of Planning

model stems from four fundamental questions which Tyler suggested must be answered in connection with any curriculum:

1. What educational purposes should the school seek to attain?
2. What educational experiences can be provided that are likely to attain these purposes?
3. How can these educational experiences be effectively organized?
4. How can we determine whether these purposes are being attained?

This gives rise to a very simple four stage model:

1. Aims and objectives;
2. Content;
3. Organization;
4. Evaluation.

Others who follow this model have suggested slight variations of it; for example, Wheeler (1967) or Taba (1962). But they are all essentially the same model. Another very famous elaboration of the model is, of course, that of Bloom and others who produced the 'taxonomy of educational objectives'. This is a categorization of objectives which has lent much support to the use of the model, especially in the USA.

In the UK the objectives model has had only limited popularity and application. Some Schools Council curriculum projects started out using this model (for example, *Science 5-13)* but have been unable, or unwilling, to sustain the use of the model throughout the project. Only one English writer, J. E. Merritt, has put forward a pure version of the objectives model. In his book *What Shall We Teach?*, 1974, he suggested a four stage G.P.I.D model:

1. making intelligent decisions about *goals;*
2. designing adequate *plans*;
3. *implementing* these plans skilfully;
4. *developing* from the new base line that has been achieved.

A more elaborate version of Merritt's G.P.I.D. was included (1972) in the Open University course E283, Unit 10 (A.O.S.T.M.T.E.C.):

1. Aims;
2. Objectives;
3. Strategies;
4. Tactics;
5. Methods;
6. Techniques;
7. Evaluation;
8. Consolidation.

Models of Planning

It may be significant that when the Open University curriculum course was revised, this aspect of it was dropped completely.

As was shown in Ch. 8, there have been many criticisms of the objectives model, for example, Stenhouse, 1975, and Sockett, 1976. Apart from the unsuitability of applying the factory model to educational enterprises, Stenhouse argues that pre-specifying pupil responses in many school subjects is not only impracticable but actually harmful as a curriculum plan. Sockett also argues that pre-specification is undesirable since it would produce a static model of knowledge — he argues along Popperian lines that scientific thinking rests on the assumption of falsifiability.

2. The Process or Input Model

This model is often associated with the work of Stenhouse who not only objected to the product or output model, but put forward an alternative view. Stenhouse argues that in education it is more appropriate to specify content and the established principles of procedure contained within disciplines and traditions rather than specifying objectives. He suggests that the objectives model can be useful only for some low level skills and other kinds of simple learning.

The essence of the process model is that the teacher encourages pupils to explore worthwhile educational areas or processes rather than to reach certain pre-specified conclusions or to acquire certain information. The teacher needs to be confident that the enterprise is a valuable one, but not to be able to predict exactly what changes will take place, as a result, in the pupils' behaviour. This view of a teacher operating within a disciplined framework rather than with objectives has developed into 'the teacher as researcher'.

Stenhouse also suggests that for many aspects of the school curriculum no one knows the answer. It is therefore foolish to specify objectives or even, in some cases, content. What will work in one school will be a disastrous failure in another. What is required, according to Stenhouse, is an attitude of mind and a set of procedures held by the teacher. The teacher must regard his classrooom as a laboratory, in which the teacher researcher develops tentative hypotheses about techniques, materials etc. The input or process model was an important reaction against 'planning by objectives', but is it a complete curriculum model in its own right?

It might also be objected that this kind of curriculum model is splendid for developing teachers' professional skills, but leaves much to be desired in terms of national, regional or even school planning. We will need to come back to this controversy later.

3. The Situational Analysis or Cultural Analysis Model
This model is also essentially American in origin, although it has been modified considerably in its English versions. Smith, Stanley and Shores (1957) in *Fundamentals of Curriculum Development* and Broudy, Smith and Burnett (1964) *Democracy and Excellence in American Secondary Education*, put forward a view of curriculum based on the idea of common culture and common curriculum. In the UK Raymond Williams in his book *The Long Revolution*, 1961, came to remarkably similar conclusions, although there is no evidence that he was aware of this American tradition.

Skilbeck's curriculum model is essentially eclectic and includes some aspects of both the objectives approach and the process model. He refers to his model as situational analysis. Skilbeck acknowledges that the curriculum is essentially value laden and political in character. Nevertheless, individual schools have to come to terms with the social context of the school and plan a curriculum accordingly. The best version of Skilbeck's model is contained in the Open University course E203, Unit 8. A much more detailed version can be found in Reynolds and Skilbeck, *Culture and the Classroom*, 1976.

Another version of this approach is contained in Lawton *et al.* (1978). The advantage of the cultural analysis model is that whereas the objectives model is too much dependent on an industrial psychology view, and the process model perhaps too much influenced by philosophy, cultural analysis is essentially multidisciplinary (see diagram).

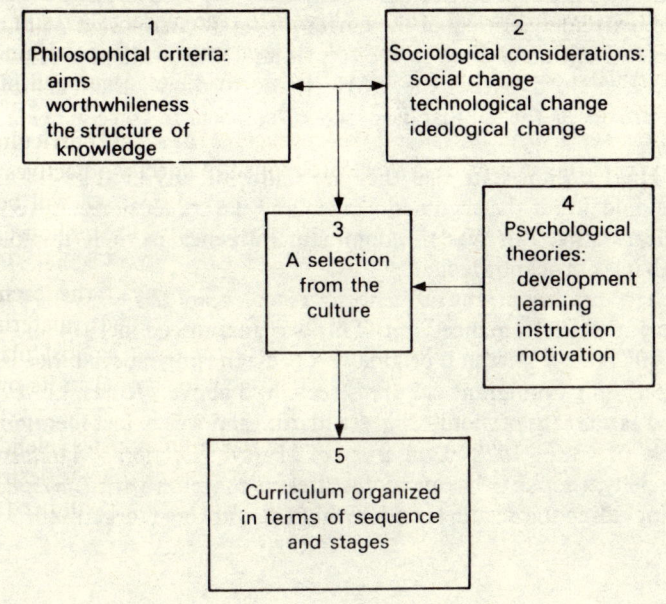

```
┌─────────────────────────┐      ┌─────────────────────────┐
│           1             │      │           2             │
│ Philosophical criteria: │◄────►│ Sociological considerations:│
│   aims                  │      │   social change         │
│   worthwhileness        │      │   technological change  │
│   the structure of      │      │   ideological change    │
│     knowledge           │      │                         │
└─────────────────────────┘      └─────────────────────────┘
                │                              │
                │                              │
                ▼                    ┌─────────────────────┐
         ┌──────────────┐            │          4          │
         │      3       │            │    Psychological    │
         │ A selection  │◄───────────│     theories:       │
         │  from the    │            │   development       │
         │   culture    │            │   learning          │
         └──────────────┘            │   instruction       │
                │                    │   motivation        │
                │                    └─────────────────────┘
                ▼
      ┌───────────────────────┐
      │           5           │
      │ Curriculum organized  │
      │ in terms of sequence  │
      │     and stages        │
      └───────────────────────┘
```

Models of Planning

The logic of the cultural analysis model demands that we look at society as it is now (and as it is developing) as well as examining the curriculum of the past, and trying to plot trends of development. If we ask what kind of society we live in (as well as what kind of society we want) then the two major features which stand out are that we are a democratic society and a scientific and technological society. This clearly has implications for the content of the curriculum.

The fact that we are a democratic society not only has implications for 'who should be educated' but also about the content of the curriculum. Many would argue, and I would be one of them, that the logic of comprehensive secondary education leads to a view of curriculum based on a common culture. This makes the cultural analysis model essential for a society where not only is knowledge changing, but also values and ideologies. This model of curriculum planning is essentially concerned with questions about the kind of knowledge and the kinds of educational experiences which everyone ought to have in our kind of democratic society. It is concerned with what kind of knowledge is necessary for people as workers, as citizens and as creative human beings.

One practical implication of this curriculum model has emerged in recent years in the form of the HMI discussion document *Curriculum 11-16*, 1977 (see Ch. 4 above). In this context there are three interesting features of this proposed curriculum. The first is that it advocates a common curriculum for the compulsory secondary school age range, using about 75 per cent of the time available for pupils. The second is that HMI are extremely critical of the current form of curriculum planning by means of option choices in the fourth and fifth years of secondary schools. The third is that the HMI choose to model their common curriculum not on the familiar list of school 'subjects' but on eight *kinds of experience*.

The HMI do not state that they are following any kind of cultural analysis model, but the arguments given and the conclusions arrived at show clearly that this was the dominant influence in their thinking, although it is not acknowledged.

Another very important influence in recent years has been the DES Assessment of Performance Unit. This was announced in 1974 and set up in 1975 as a method originally of diagnosing special needs — particularly for immigrant children (see Ch. 8 above.) It has, however, emerged as a means of monitoring standards (and was in fact mentioned as such in the 1979 Conservative Party Election Manifesto). Superficially, the APU has many features in common with *Curriculum 11-16*, including the headings under which monitoring is organized:

Kinds of Development (APU)   *Area of Experience (Curriculum 11-16)*

Kinds of Development (APU)	Area of Experience (Curriculum 11-16)
Language	Linguistic
Mathematics	Mathematical
Science	Scientific
Social and Personal	Social and Political
Aesthetic	Aesthetic and Creative
Physical	Physical
	Ethical
	Spiritual

But there are two important differences between this model and the common curriculum outlined in *Curriculum 11-16*. The first is that the model behind APU is a developmental model: the six headings are called 'kinds of development'. This combined with the fact that tests are to be devised for each of these six 'kinds of development', makes the model here more like an objectives model than a cultural analysis model.

The testing programme is fraught with all sorts of methodological difficulties, including the Rasch model and the whole question of item banking. Those concerned with the development of the APU have promised and reassured teachers that 'backwash' onto the curriculum from the testing would be minimal. In practice, however, the backwash is likely to be very considerable, especially if LEAs also get involved in similar testing programmes based not on 'light sampling' but on 'blanket testing'.

Both of these recent developments have been mentioned at this stage to illustrate the fact that curriculum theory is not confined to abstract questions, but necessarily gets involved with very practical issues about what is happening in schools. Teachers need to be particularly well informed in order to examine carefully both the suggestions made in *Curriculum 11-16*, and also the kinds of tests which will be employed as a result of the APU programme. One of the surprising features of the APU is that it has received so little publicity and has caused almost no controversy in the last five years. But all sorts of questions need to be asked about the kind of objectives/development model in use. For example, what is the philosophical justification for the six kinds of development? What is the sociological reason for not including either politics or technology? Surely, both must be regarded as important kinds of knowledge in our society today. What has been presented as uncontroversial is in reality shot through with all sorts of curriculum problems.

Models of Planning

FURTHER READING

An interesting philosophical approach to curriculum planning and design is contained in Hugh Sockett's *Designing the Curriculum,* 1976. It includes a chapter on objectives. Although it is about the USA, Broudy, Smith and Burnett, 1964, is essential reading for those concerned with the common culture/common curriculum idea.

QUESTIONS
1. What is wrong with planning a curriculum by listing behavioural objectives?
2. Discuss the similarities and differences between the eight 'areas of experience' *(Curriculum 11-16)* and the six 'kinds of development' (APU).

11
Cognition and Curriculum 1: The Primary Years
Maggie Ing

Psychological theories of learning and development are important in curriculum planning in at least two ways. *Models* of curriculum planning contain assumptions about the nature of learning; and the *design* of particular curriculum projects frequently prescribes an ideal of 'good learning' and may rest upon a theory of learners' typical development. In the case of the objectives model of curriculum, the link with behaviourist psychology is clear and overt, while the process and cultural analysis models have an affinity with cognitive theories. The fit between curriculum and psychological models is not always exact, but it is important to examine the adequacy of the theoretical underpinnings of plans which may be translated into policy.

We have as yet no comprehensive and agreed theory of cognitive development. There are theories and, several paces behind, empirical studies, in profusion, but as Ausubel (1968) acknowledges: 'Unfortunately, however, it must be admitted that at the present time this discipline can only offer a limited number of very crude generalizations and highly tentative suggestions'. Yet theories of cognitive development have been embodied in curriculum plans, particularly in primary schools.

Piaget and the Geneva School
Despite the widespeard influence of Piaget's mapping of stages in cognitive development, particularly in mathematico-logical reasoning, his work in many ways is not a suitable basis for curriculum planning. This is partly because his methodology is less than rigorous. His theories, however cogent and persuasive, are based on illustrative data from small numbers of children and he did not attempt to ensure that they were representative; subsequent attempts to verify his stages have shown that, at least so far as the age-levels attached to different stages go, they were not (e.g. Peel, 1959, Lunzer, 1960, Elkind, 1961). No statistical analysis of data is offered. His clinical interview technique, which can be a very

sensitive method of obtaining information, is vulnerable to criticism; conditions were not standardized for all the subjects, and it is quite possible that leading questions were responsible for at least some of the answers obtained. The usual precautions of laying down clear criteria for classifying responses, and checking that different raters agreed amongst themselves, were not taken. Ideally, the best way of demonstrating the growth of children's thought would not be by comparing the responses of different age-groups of different children, but by longitudinal studies of the same children.

These omissions would make most of his work inadmissible as social science, but Piaget was not attempting to function as an experimental psychologist. We might not go so far as Ausubel (1968) '...the psychological plausibility and freshness of the general outlines of his theory tend to become engulfed by a welter of logical gymnastics and abstruse, disorganized speculation', but it is fair to say that the monumental mass of his epistemological theory is in sharp contrast with the insubstantiality of his empirical data.

This is not the only reason for caution in attempting to plan a curriculum in accordance with his stages. Even the most strictly controlled research into development is 'pure' rather than 'applied' and needs some mediating theory before it can be converted into principles for action. The main interest of Piaget and his colleagues is in the structures of knowledge as demonstrated by children's growing powers. Consequently, important questions for *education* — what *can* we teach children, what *should* we teach (a question not answerable solely by any account of development), *how* can we intervene to promote transition from stage to stage, either to ensure normal learning or to remedy inadequate learning or to accelerate learning? — are not the province of 'pure' theories, though any answers will certainly draw upon such theories.

Piaget's theories are essentially concerned with *structure*. They set out to describe the characteristics of hypothesized invariant steps of human mental functioning. In schools, we are concerned with individuals who rarely fit neatly into stage-categories even in one subject-area, and certainly not in their performance across the whole curriculum.

The vast body of research stemming from Piaget's work has to date shown the complexity and lack of consistency in the ways in which we attain intelligent, rational thought.

> Despite progressive refinements of method aimed at removing from the experimental data all variation due to extraneous factors, the most striking feature of the results of these studies is the degree of inter- and intra-individual variability obtained.
>
> J. G. WALLACE, in Varma and Williams (1976).

It is true that Piaget has tried to accommodate these variations into his theory, e.g. with the concepts of horizontal and vertical decalage; and that Flavell and Wohlwill (1969) have proposed a model of development which tried to encompass situational and individual variables. But these amplifications of the original theory are of little direct help to teachers, except insofar as they remind us of what we already know, that cognitive growth is *not* simple and uniform even in a single child.

Bruner: the Processes of Cognitive Growth
By contrast with the Genevan School, J. S. Bruner is much more interested in the *processes* of cognitive growth than the structure of intelligence at different stages. Piaget's (1967) contention that Bruner has not really presented a 'theory' is quite fair. But Bruner's conclusions about some vital aspects of cognition, based on his own and many other research studies, have a direct bearing on curriculum planning. He seems to accept the basic Piagetian model, as his inclusion (1960) of a lengthy quotation from Piaget's colleague B. Inhelder shows. The main points he accepts are:

1. The most elementary forms of reasoning have their roots in *the principle of the invariance of quantities.*
2. Children arrive at the invariance principle only after a long period of concrete experience. Initially, numbers, spatial dimensions and other physical quantities are not perceived as constant, but capable of change.
3. Children often focus on only one aspect of a phenomenon at one time.
4. The sequence of cognitive development often follows more closely the inherent *logical* order of a subject than its historical development.

From these observations of children's thinking, Inhelder makes direct suggestions for the curriculum of primary schools.

1. A teaching method that takes into account the natural thought processes will allow the child to discover such principles of invariance by giving him an opportunity to progress beyond his own primitive mode of thinking through confrontation by concrete data...
2. Concrete activity that becomes increasingly formal is what leads the child to the kind of mental mobility that approaches the naturally reversible operations of mathematics and logic.
3. We can set up little teaching experiments in such a way that he is

forced to pay attention to other aspects.
4. ...it is possible to draw up methods of teaching the basic ideas in science and mathematics to children considerably younger than the traditional age. It is at this earlier age that systematic instruction can lay a groundwork in the fundamentals that can be used later and with great profit at the secondary level.

Her vision of a possible mathematics and science curriculum for the first two years of school (which would be from 6-8 years old) is not unfamiliar to many Infant or First School teachers: 'One wonders in the light of all this whether it might not be interesting to devote the first two years of school to a series of exercises in manipulating, classifying, and ordering objects in ways that highlight basic operations of logical addition, multiplication, inclusion, serial ordering, and the like.' (in Bruner, 1966).

Modes of Representation

Although Bruner takes as his basis the stages outlined by Piaget and Inhelder, particularly in mathematical and logical reasoning, he adds (1966) his model of the three basic *modes* of representing reality—enactive, iconic and symbolic. Although these modes develop sequentially, all three are present long before school age, and their interaction, or the dominance of any one, is partly attributable to the task in hand, as well as to developmental level and individual cognitive style.

There are three kinds of representational systems that are operative during the growth of human intellect and whose interaction is central to growth. All of them are amenable to specification in fairly precise terms, all can be shown to be affected and shaped by linkage with tool or instrumental systems, all of them are within important limits affected by cultural conditioning and by man's evolution. They are, as already indicated, enactive representation, iconic representation, and symbolic representation—knowing something through doing it, through a picture or image of it, and through some such symbolic means as language. The job of the teacher is *not* to hasten progress from mode to mode, but to nourish the development of all three: 'I am convinced that we shall do better to conceive of growth as an empowering of the individual by multiple means for representing his world, multiple means that often conflict and create the dilemmas that stimulate growth.' (Bruner, 1974).

The Spiral Curriculum

From his view of cognitive development, he adopts an optimistic approach to curriculum planning. Children may be unable to understand in the final codified, adult versions the essential principles of knowledge, but they are capable of grasping *at their own level* the essence of knowledge. The primary school curriculum can, and *should*, deal with the most important knowledge and values of society.

If one respects the ways of thought of the growing child, if one is courteous enough to translate material into his logical forms and challenging enough to tempt him to advance, then it is possible to introduce him at an early age to the ideas and styles that in later life make an educated man. We might ask, as a criterion for any subject taught in primary school, whether, when fully developed, it is worth an adult's knowing, and whether having known it as a child makes a person a better adult. (Bruner, 1966).

What Bruner advocates is not any specific curriculum for the primary school, but a set of guiding principles upon which the curriculum should be based. Briefly, these are:

1. that the central concepts of knowledge should be translated into activities within the capacities of children.
2. that *systematic* re-introduction to those concepts should bring children to develop increasingly powerful mental strategies.
3. that these ends are best achieved by the *active* involvement of children in generating their own schemata.
   and
4. that the three modes of representing reality should all be developed by education.

In many ways, Bruner's suggestions are close to a process model of curriculum, but he lays stress also on *knowledge* and the importance of careful re-structuring of concepts, a view compatible with the cultural analysis model.

Ausubel: the importance of language
So far as school learning is concerned, the symbolic mode is easily the most important for D. P. Ausubel. He stresses the role of language and meaning at all levels of learning, and, although sometimes guilty of demolishing straw men (no one, for instance, would argue that all primary education *should* be conducted on 'an intuitive, problem-solving (discovery), and nonverbal basis', Ausubel, 1968), he does usefully set out a justification of traditional school practice. Like Bruner, he takes Piaget's stages as his starting-point, but rejects some of the conclusions which have been drawn from them. He makes the distinction between *primary concepts*, 'whose meanings a given individual originally learns in

relation to genuine concrete-empirical experience', and *secondary concepts*, 'whose criterial attributes yield generic meanings during learning when they (the attributes) are related to his cognitive structures *without* being first explicitly related to the particular exemplars from which they are derived'. Children at the pre-operational stage of development he sees as constrained by their inability to use secondary concepts, and equates this stage with the pre-school period, although it probably holds good for many infant school children in this country where schooling begins earlier than in most others.

During the concrete operational stage, which covers most of the primary school years, 'the child is capable of acquiring secondary abstractions and of understanding, using, and meaningfully manipulating both *secondary* abstractions and the relations between them'. He is no longer dependent on 'genuine concrete-empirical experience', but on *concrete-empirical props,* which are themselves abstractions from experience. Such props need not be tangible; 'words that represent particular exemplars or attributes of a concept are very adequate concrete-empirical props'.

Although the child's thinking becomes increasingly more efficient, there are still constraints:

> ...where complex propositions are involved, he is largely restricted to an intuitive or semi-abstract level of cognitive functioning, a level that falls far short of the clarity, precision, explicitness and generality associated with the more advanced abstract stage of intellectual development.

Ausubel disagrees with Piaget's contention that the child's thinking at this stage is closely tied to concrete experience. 'The concreteness of this stage inheres rather, in the fact that secondary abstractions and the relationships between them can be understood and meaningfully manipulated *only* with the aid of current or recent concrete-empirical props.' The child is, in effect, functioning in a way much closer to the abstract logical stage of development than to the pre-operational stage.

Structure and the Curriculum

Ausubel and Bruner differ mainly in their pedagogical prescriptions; their curriculum recommendations are remarkably close. Both are much concerned with the *structure* of what is to be learned, but Bruner's view of the processes of cognition lead him to conclude that the best learning takes place when the learner *discovers* structure. Ausubel regards that as inefficient; in his view, meaningful instruction is the most powerful and convenient teaching strategy.

The only essential condition during this period for the reception learning of propositions embodying secondary concepts is the availability of specific exemplars of the concepts in question, and such exemplars may be purely verbal in nature. Didactic exposition with such verbal props can easily be combined with other concrete-empirical props in the form of demonstrations, and usually suffices for the presentation of most subject matter that is neither excessively complex nor excessively unfamiliar.

Neither Bruner nor Ausubel sees any need to restrict the primary school curriculum to fundamental intellectual skills, though each argues from different premises. Bruner holds that knowledge can be adapted to the child, Ausubel that the child's 'cognitive equipment is certainly adequate enough for acquiring an intuitive grasp of many concepts in the basic disciplines'. Ausubel, however, does not agree that we can, or should, attempt to teach *any* subject to *any* child: '...the concept of the spiral curriculum...is eminently sound provided an attempt is *not* made to teach at an intuitive level "reduced" versions of *anything* or *everything* presented later at a more abstract level'. (Not that Bruner ever suggested that we should.)

Some concepts, he claims, are too difficult to translate; others need prior knowledge that the primary school child is unlikely to have acquired; and some become useless when restructured in intuitive terms.

Conclusion

From this brief examination of three influential theories of cognitive development, it can be seen that there is no clear consensus either about the pattern of children's emerging abilities, or about the best educational strategies to adopt. Hard, empirical evidence is lacking, especially in areas other than mathematics. The whole picture is complicated, not only by individual differences *between* children, but by differences in the *same* children's abilities in different sorts of task. It is theoretically possible for broad lines of development in every area of knowledge to be drawn up. This sort of normative information could be useful, provided that it would not be inflexibly applied either to curriculum planning or to assessment. Such facts as we have about cognitive growth suggest the need to allow for different rates of development, and for a variety of ways of learning.

FURTHER READING
J. Piaget and B. Inhelder, *The Psychology of the Child*, 1969. An overview of Piaget's work, essential reading for anyone seriously interested in his theory.

Cognition and Curriculum I: The Primary Years

J. Turner, *Cognitive Development*, 1975. A short but surprisingly comprehensive survey of theories and empirical studies. Useful as an initial *reference* book for students not versed in psychology, but some knowledge of psychology is probably necessary to read it through.

J. S. Bruner, *Studies in Cognitive Growth*, 1965, Chapters 1 and 2. Fairly difficult, but the most comprehensive statement of his theory of cognitive development.

QUESTIONS
1. How far do you agree that theories of cognitive development 'can only offer a limited number of very crude generalizations and highly tentative suggestions'?
2. Discuss the differences between the theories of Bruner and Ausubel and their implications for the primary school curriculum.

12
Cognition and Curriculum II: Adolescence and Beyond
Maggie Ing

Despite the criticisms of Piaget and the Geneva School and the reservations about the appropriateness of their theories for curriculum planning summarized in the previous chapter, it seems sensible to begin with their account of the final stage of cognitive development, because it has dominated subsequent studies.

From 11 to 12 years of age, a new mode of reasoning is acquired. The child is no longer limited to dealing with objects of direct representation of reality, but becomes able to use 'hypotheses', that is, he can respond to the *logic* of propositions irrespective of their *content*. New operations are added to his repertoire; *implications* (if...then); *disjunctions* (either... or); incompatibilities; and conjunctions. The new operations can be combined and inverted, so that the child is capable of using all the basic logical transformations.

A brief summary of the logical characteristics of formal operational thought can be found in Piaget, 1971, pp.33-4, and for those undaunted by technicality, a full exposition can be found in Inhelder and Piaget, 1958.

Ausubel and the Secondary Curriculum
Ausubel, 1968, slightly reformulates the hypothesized new skills of pupils of secondary school age:

> Eventually, after sufficient gradual change in this direction, a qualitatively new capacity emerges: the intellectually mature individual becomes capable of understanding and manipulating relationships between abstractions without any reference whatsoever to concrete-empirical reality.

The pupil becomes 'an abstract verbal learner', 'ready at the secondary school level for a new type of verbal expository teaching that uses particular examples primarily for *illustrative* purposes'. Ausubel concedes that concrete-empirical props are still sometimes useful in enabling learning in new areas, but for the great part of adolescent learning he is firmly convinced that abstract, verbal teaching is not only more efficient, economically, but also more efficient in terms of understanding. Verbal understanding, he claims, is more easily transferable to new situations.

No one would wish to deny the power and economy of language in the organization, retention and manipulation of knowledge and thought. But one might question the extreme position of Ausubel on two grounds. First, is it equally suitable for all *tasks* (skills, for example, including higher-order skills, may be better learned for some degree of verbal exposition, but surely require performance, rehearsal and a clear model of the end product to a much greater extent), and, second, is it equally suitable for all pupils? The traditional grammar school pedagogy seems to fit Ausubel's ideal, but it could not be said to have developed the powers of all, or even the majority, of the pupils receiving it.

His views on the secondary school curriculum are easier to agree with. He recommends 'serious and solid academic fare' and rightly inveighs against trivial, time-wasting school courses. Given his theory of the *potential* of pupils, he may well be right in complaining that 'very little has been done in the way of providing the student with a meaningful, integrated and systematic view of the major ideas in a given field of knowledge'.

While he sees *breadth* of curriculum as particularly appropriate for the primary school child, who is a 'generalist' in that his intellect and personality are relatively underdeveloped and consequently need introductions to many different fields of knowledge, *depth* of curriculum assumes importance in secondary schools when the student is ready for more intensive and more specialized study. 'Depth' refers to the greater complexity of knowlege that should be available, not to the degree of autonomy the student should be expected to exercise in its pursuit.

> If the secondary school student is required to discover most principles autonomously, to obtain most subject-matter content from primary sources, and to design his own experiments, he has time to acquire only methodological sophistication...
> D. P. AUSUBEL, (1968).

One wonders where the secondary schools making such requirements are to be found; I suspect that verbal exposition is by far the most common means of instruction and the exposure of pupils to primary sources and their own devices extremely rare.

Problems and Limitations of Developmental Theory

If our knowledge of the cognitive development of children before adolescence, despite an awesome wealth of experimental study, is too general to be translated into curriculum practice, the same failure is even more true of studies of older children. Not only is there a dearth of detailed research, but the grouping together of the thought-processes of children from about 11 and those of adults of obviously different capacities, seems at variance with common sense. 'As every teacher will readily confirm, the actual picture obtained of the growth of thinking in a class of pupils is far less simple than Piaget's model would seem to imply' (Peel, 1971).

Piaget is concerned with the emergence of *logical reasoning,* which represents only *one* form of thinking, and, even so, is not to be found consistently amongst able and highly-educated adults. What he provides is an ideal model of the culmination of typical stages of the development of rationality, not an accurate representation of how real people behave in situations. 'Ideal' does not here mean a goal to be sought, but a 'pure' theoretical construct. To assume that his description characterizes all secondary school children is to fall into the trap satirically expressed by Richmond (1971):

> Eventually this detachment from the senses becomes total and he attains the 'symbolic' level where he is at last free to enjoy the combinatorial power of rational thought, to inhabit a stratosphere where all the baser passions have been left behind, and where all his subjective hunches are transcended by his mastery of the strategies of problem-solving.

Richmond goes on to make two serious points — that individuals *vary* in their own ways of learning, and that many of our curriculum concerns are not to be fitted into the pattern of logical reasoning:

> Even where the strategies for mathematical-logical-problem-solving are fully worked out, the task analysis complete down to the last detail, and the structure and sequence of the courses to be followed tolerably well-known in advance, the fact is that each and every individual has his own preferences...If this is true of symbolic procedures, it is reasonable to suppose that it is true to an even greater extent in those mental activities where mathematical-logical structures either do not apply or prove unhelpful. *(ibid.)*

Cognition and Curriculum II: Adolescence and Beyond

Logic and Lack of Logic in Adult Thinking

Whether or not pupils of secondary school age *can* use abstract modes of thinking from the ages of 11 or 12, it is certain that neither adolescents nor adults *do* think in logical ways in all situations in which they might be appropriate.

We have at present an incomplete map of the total structure of mature and maturing thought. Piaget and his colleagues have explored three main features:

1. the data of formal thought (i.e. symbolic and abstract content)
2. the operation of formal thinking (ie. the ability to form classes and relationships and handle transformations)
3. the structure of propositional reasoning (i.e. the *logical* as opposed to *psychological* features of reasoning).

To these, Peel (1968) adds

4. the strategies of reasoning

as an area of research which gives significant leads to consideration of the development of the powers of thought. Two studies, both with adult subjects, reflect some of the complex mixture of logic and illogic in just *one* aspect of cognition, the acquisition of concepts.

Concept acquisition

1. Bruner, Goodnow and Austin (1968) created experimental situations in which the strategies used by their subjects to attain conjunctive and disjunctive concepts were revealed. The experimental design for reception strategies (where the subject does not control the instances given him — a parallel of real-life experiences) will serve as an illustration.

The materials used were 81 cards, printed with different figures and borders, in the possible combinations shown below:

Attribute	Colour	Type of Figure	No. of Figures	Border
	Green	Cross	1	Single
	or	or	or	or
	Black	Circle	2	Double
	or	or	or	or
	Red	Square	3	Treble

Single conjunctive concepts would be 'all black figures'; 'all cards with a green square and a single border'. The subjects, undergraduate students, were told that they had to discover the concept and the only information they were given was whether each card turned up was or was not an instance.

From the logical possibilities of the task, and the behaviour of the successful problem-solvers, Bruner worked out two 'ideal strategies' of *focusing* and *scanning*. Individuals showed consistent preferences for one rather than the other. 'Focusing' involves taking the first positive instance in its entirety as the initial hypothesis; this is highly economic of effort as the subject only needs to change the original hypothesis when he meets a contradictory positive instance.

	Positive Instance of concept	Negative Instance of concept
Confirms hypothesis	Keep hypothesis	Keep hypothesis
Contradicts hypothesis	Change hypothesis to what old hypothesis and new instance have in common	Theoretically impossible!

'Scanning' makes greater demands on memory and involves more guess-work, as only *part* of the first positive instance is taken as the initial hypothesis.

	Positive Instance of hypothesis	Negative Instance of hypothesis
Confirms hypothesis	Keep hypothesis	Keep hypothesis
Contradicts hypothesis	Change hypothesis to one consistent with instances so far	Change hypothesis to one consistent with instances so far

If the 'scanner' makes a lucky guess, he can arrive at the solution more quickly than the 'focuser', but on average this strategy did not pay off so well. Both stick less closely to the 'ideal' models when the tasks become more difficult. Conjunctive concepts were easily attained by most of the subjects, but disjunctive concepts, where positive instances may have no defining attributes in common (an example given by Bruner is 'allergy producers' which may be as different as chalk dust and cat fur) proved extremely difficult.

2. Wason (1966) again using undergraduate subjects, tested the strategies used in a brilliantly simple task. The subjects were told that the three numbers 2, 4, 6 formed an example of a simple relational rule which they

had to discover by generating their own examples and being told by the experimenter whether or not they had given an instance of the rule. They were told not to announce the rule until they were 'highly confident' that they had got it right and, unlike the Bruner *et al.* experiment, they kept a record of their sequences and hypotheses. (The rule was 'any increasing series of numbers'.) The most interesting result was not that most of the subjects eventually solved the problem, but that most of them sought only for *positive instances* and confidently announced the wrong rules. Even when financial penalties were exacted for incorrect guesses, the only effect was to increase the number of positive instances generated before the rule was stated. No differences, on an admittedly small sample, were found between the sexes nor between students with arts and science qualifications.

These two studies are suggestive rather than conclusive, but they point to the fact that even cognitively mature persons do not always think as logically as they might.

E. A. Peel — Adolescent Judgment

Peel (1971) has studied the reasoning of secondary school children in their forming of judgments over a range of problems closely related to the tasks we expect them to perform in the classroom.

His earlier book (1968) sets out more generally his view of cognitive growth, which owes much to Piaget but relates realistically to children in school. Although he does not formally divide the secondary school period into two or three stages, he is well aware that pupils' powers change considerably from early to middle and late adolescence. The change he sees as arising from experience:

> If concrete thinking is associated with description, then formal thought is equivalent to explanation. When the pupil is able to explain, a new quality is present in his thinking. It is the ability to jump ahead of the material evidence before him, to suggest a hypothesis and then to test it out against the material data. Hypotheses do not spring out of nothing and hence the importance of plenty of previous practical and concrete experience...

The curriculum for the first two years of secondary schooling should therefore be adapted to suit children who are not suddenly different creatures, by virtue of six or seven weeks' summer holiday, from those they were at the top of the primary school. In mathematics, concrete experience is still necessary; in science, results will typically be described rather than explained, and chemistry and biology with their predominantly concrete empirical modes of procedure often have more appeal than the abstractions of physics; languages are best learned by the concrete structure of simple correspondence because 'it is fruitless in the early stages of secondary education to attempt a logical linguistic formal explanation.' *(ibid.)*

None of this is new or startling and is already common practice, or at least common intention, in our secondary schools. The more original part of Peel's work is his (1971) investigation of adolescent judgment. He does not claim that this is a comprehensive account of cognition, but it is certainly one of the most important aspects of thinking, particularly as the secondary school curriculum in all areas from mathematics to moral education has shifted emphasis from delivering information and requiring only rehearsal and retention to attempting to involve pupils in comparison, problem-solving, discussion and hypothesis-making. Moreover, he sees the mental powers of adolescents not solely in terms of propositional reasoning but in the wider context of increased awareness, idealism and creativity:

> Above all else the adolescent and young adult apprehend the inconsistencies between the actual and the possible. They are impelled to the opinion and action which characterizes their lives by a drive to reconcile this actuality of their existence with the possibilities they themselves envisage. Usually, they strive to modify the actual. This going forward and outward to conceive of possibilities beyond the limits of their environment is the central feature of their intellectual life.

The intellectual processes involved in this capacity are *understanding* and *judgement*, both of which reveal themselves at different levels. Understanding has a variety of meanings, which Peel summarizes as 'understanding a reasoned discourse in terms of cause-and-effect relations, seeing a problem in terms of high-level concepts, sensitivity to formal relations and a capacity to follow deductive argument'. Although it is an important part of education, understanding is not enough. We need to develop effective judgments by which we select our course of action, particularly where there is no single correct course.

It is not possible to summarize with any justice Peel's theoretical analysis of judgment, discussion of the relevant literature and range of meticulous empirical investigations. One example can merely give the flavour of the book, which should be read in its entirety.

Pupils aged 11-14+ were given the following passage and questions:

Lynn is a large town with a busy railway junction which attracts boys who are interested in train-spotting. Burton is a small place not far away and so many people who live there do their shopping in Lynn because there are more shops. British Railways have recently decided to close Burton station and run no more trains from there to Lynn.
Q. Should Burton station be closed?
Q. Why do you say that?

PEEL (1971)

The answers to the questions were graded in three categories, in increasing levels of maturity of judgment:
1. restricted (e.g. Yes. One day a train spotter may get killed).
2. circumstantial (e.g. No. The people of Burton may depend on Lynn for their shopping).
3. imaginative-comprehensive (e.g. It depends on whether many people use the train and if they have other ways of travelling to Lynn).

The results of this and other passages and problems indicated that level 1 responses were made by only a few of the youngest children; level 2, logical but restricted to the information given, was the almost universal response of pupils of 13-14 years; whereas level 3 was not typical until about 15+. Although the ability, experience and sophistication of pupils makes for an earlier acquisition of level 3, Peel believes that there may be a maturational factor involved, as it does not seem to emerge before about 14 years.

Peel goes beyond eliciting and classifying pupils' judgments to discuss the possibility of promoting mature judgments. Multiple-choice answers gave rise to better judgments than open-ended questions, a finding which echoes other studies (e.g. Mosher 1962, quoted by Bruner, 1974) showing that children can *recognize* better strategies than those they spontaneously generate. This has important pedagogical implications: 'The essence of the process is that of a free exchange of ideas and material between pupil and teacher with an optimum load of responsibility being placed on the thinker for solving his own problems'. (Peel, 1971).

Conclusion

The inferences that can be drawn from the present state of our knowledge of cognitive development, especially development in the secondary school years, are bound to seem slight, even trite, to sensitive and committed teachers. Indeed, I believe that theorists could learn much from the good practice of such teachers. This is not to recommend an anti-intellectual stance, but to point out that we need a powerful and comprehensive theory of intellectual growth, developed through *co-ordinated* empirical data.

Nonetheless, what does emerge from the more accessible sources of theory and information is that the secondary school curriculum should aim at some balance of imparting knowledge of increasing depth and rigour, by developing understanding by *all* appropriate means, and of giving pupils the chance to exercise and increase their powers of judgment. Whether this can be achieved within areas of knowledge alone, or whether special courses in 'thinking' would be generally transferable is just one of the many unanswered (but not inherently unanswerable) questions we are currently faced with. The emphasis on 'understanding' and the link between increased powers of thought and maturing *affective* concerns, brought out by Peel, argue against the behavioural objectives model of curriculum, but fit either the process or cultural analysis models.

FURTHER READING

E. A. Lunzer and J. F. Morris, *Development in Learning,* 1968, Vol. 2, Chs. 8, 10 and 14. Technical, but an excellent source book.

E. A. Peel, 'The Thinking and Education of the Adolescent', in V. P. Varma and P. Williams, eds., *Piaget, Psychology and Education,* 1976. A good, short account of Peel's work.

QUESTIONS

1. How far does our present knowledge of cognitive development support the contention that our pupils have enough in common to follow a common curriculum?
2. By what means would you seek to promote a) understanding and b) judgment in your pupils in any particular area of knowledge?

13
Theories of Instruction
Maggie Ing

Theories of instruction have their roots in value assumptions and seek to apply models, concepts and empirical information from psychology directly to the task of education. They are part of a growing body of specifically educational psychology, which can be distinguished from its parent body by its focus of inquiry and its practical, *prescriptive* purpose. (For a fuller discussion, see Ausubel, 1968, Ch. 1.) Theories of instruction seek to prescribe both the arrangement and presentation of knowledge and the management of learning. The theories of Bruner and Gagné provide an interesting contrast. Both are linked to an objectives model of curriculum, but Bruner's permits of a wide definition of 'objectives', while Gagné's is strongly linked to *behavioural* objectives.

Bruner's Theory of Instruction
Towards a Theory of Instruction (1966) as its title indicates, does not claim to present a fully worked-out theory. In his rapid eclectic style, Bruner generates a multitude of ideas, presented but not totally pursued. He does, however, specify clearly the components which any theory of instruction *ought* to have. It should be *prescriptive*, (though deriving in part from *descriptive* theories of learning and development) and set forth rules for effective learning. The rules can in turn provide a standard for evaluating any particular way of teaching or learning. It should also be *normative,* setting up criteria and the conditions for meeting them, of a high degree of generality. There are four major areas in which it should guide and inform practice:

1. PREDISPOSITIONS
We need to know which experiences predispose individuals towards learning in general, and particular types of learning. These would include cultural, motivational and personal factors. He gives the example of the predisposition to explore alternatives and alludes to research on exploratory behaviour which indicates the importance of an optimal level of uncertainty to spark off curiosity.

2. STRUCTURE

We need to know the ways in which a body of knowledge should be structured so that it can most easily be learned by individuals. Optimal structures relate both to the capabilities of the learner and to the 'deep structures' of the knowledge itself. It is in this area that Bruner has made his most distinctive contribution to curriculum planning. His idea of the 'spiral curriculum', in which the central concepts of knowledge are introduced, then re-introduced, to learners in forms appropriate to their developing mental powers, is potentially one of the most important principles for education that has emerged in the last 20 years. That it has not more extensively been put into practice is probably a reflection on the way in which educational resources are allocated. It would involve the collaboration of the best minds in different branches of knowledge, in practical teaching and in the field of cognitive development. Bruner himself showed how it could be done in mathematics with Z.P. Dienes the eminent mathematician (see Bruner, 1966, pp. 56-72).

3. SEQUENCE

We need to know the most effective sequences in which to present what is to be learned. Sequence, like structure, will be relative to the learner as well as to the internal logic of the knowledge. It is not always a matter of going from simple to complex. 'Look-and-say' and phonic methods of learning to read are examples of quite different principles of sequencing. The best sequence may depend also on the desired outcome of the learning — is the child to be able to decipher new words, or to build up a repertoire of words that he wants to use?

4. REINFORCEMENT

We need to know which reinforcements will enhance learning and how to pace them as learning progresses. Learning without instruction can be a haphazard process. It is partly in the timing and quality of feedback and reinforcement that the justification for instruction lies. If we know how and when to give the learner usable information about his progress, he will learn more efficiently. More than this, we need to know how to make the learner self-reinforcing in time. 'The tutor must correct the learner in a fashion that eventually makes it possible for the learner to take over the corrective function himself' (Bruner. 1966).

Bruner has never filled in the details of his theory of instruction. Like much of his writing on education, his notes are stimulating and informed by a wide range of experimental work. The theme which gives coherence to his eclectic brilliance is his emphasis on cognitive growth and processes. For him, the curriculum must be planned to amplify the powers of mind, must be concerned with *knowing* rather than merely with *knowledge*.

Gagné's Theory of Instruction
Gagné's theory of instruction cannot be criticized as unsystematic, nor neglectful of detail. Three books (Gagné, 1970 and 1974, Gagné and Briggs, 1974) set out meticulously his theoretical basis and prescriptions for action, right down to the planning of individual lessons. The emphasis, and whole flavour, of his work is very different from Bruner's. It falls into three main parts:
1. an information-processing theory of learning, together with
2. his classification of types of learning, and the best conditions for their occurence, which give rise to
3. a detailed set of rules for instruction.

Gagné's Theory of Learning
Gagné (1974) sets out explicitly the model of human learning processes which underpins his educational psychology. The human brain is assumed to work rather like a computer, coding information from the environment and transforming it. Figure 1. shows the hypothesized flow of information through the structures of the central nervous system.

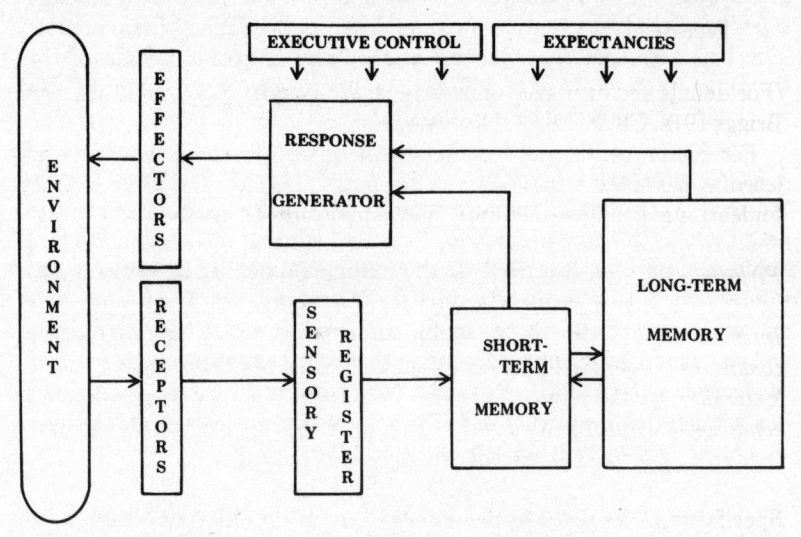

Fig. 1.
The basic model of learning and memory underlying modern 'information-processing' theories.

GAGNÉ (1974) p. 16.

The model is congruent with the present state of our knowledge of learning and of neurophysiology, though it is neither so precise nor so simple as it seems. At each stage of the process, the variables are likely to be numerous. For example, before any learning can take place, information has to be picked up by our receptors; we have, usually, to *attend* to the signals, and attention may be a function of stimulus intensity or of internal states, or both. What Gagné calls 'executive control' and 'expectancies' acknowledge the influence of the cognitive strategies and motivational states of the learner. (For a summary of Gagné's theory of learning, see Lawton *et al.*, 1978, Ch. 7.)

2. Types of Human Learning
The basic model is assumed to hold good for any act of learning. Of more immediate concern to teachers and curriculum planners is Gagné's classification of human learning into a hierarchy of increasingly complex types, from simple stimulus-response conditioning to problem-solving.

The lower levels are very simple indeed, and not normally the concern of schools, which concentrate on:

Type 5	Discriminations
Type 6	Concepts
Type 7	Rules
Type 8	Problem-solving

(For details and examples of each type, see Gagné, 1970 and Gagné and Briggs 1974, Ch. 6.)

For each type, Gagné specifies the *performance* which indicates that learning has taken place and the *internal* and *external conditions* necessary for learning. Problem-solving (type 8), for example, involves:

Performance	inventing and using a complex rule to achieve the solution of a problem which is novel to the individual
Internal conditions	in solving a problem, the learner must recall relevant subordinate rules and also relevant information.
External conditions	the learner is confronted with an actual, or represented, problem situation which he has not previously encountered. Verbal cues are minimal or absent.

Specifying *performance* leads into a setting of objectives for instruction and gives the criteria by which learning can be assessed. *Internal conditions,* i.e. the prerequisite learning, can aid diagnosis of failure to learn and form the basis of remedial instruction. *External conditions* guide the planning of instruction.

Theories of Instruction

3. Gagné's Rules for Instruction
i) LEARNING OUTCOMES

Learning types 5-8 are called by Gagné *intellectual skills* and are subsumed into his later classification (Gagné, 1974, and Gagné and Briggs, 1974) of the *learning outcomes* which he takes to be the main business of education:

1. Verbal information
2. Intellectual skill
3. Cognitive strategy
4. Attitude
5. Motor skill

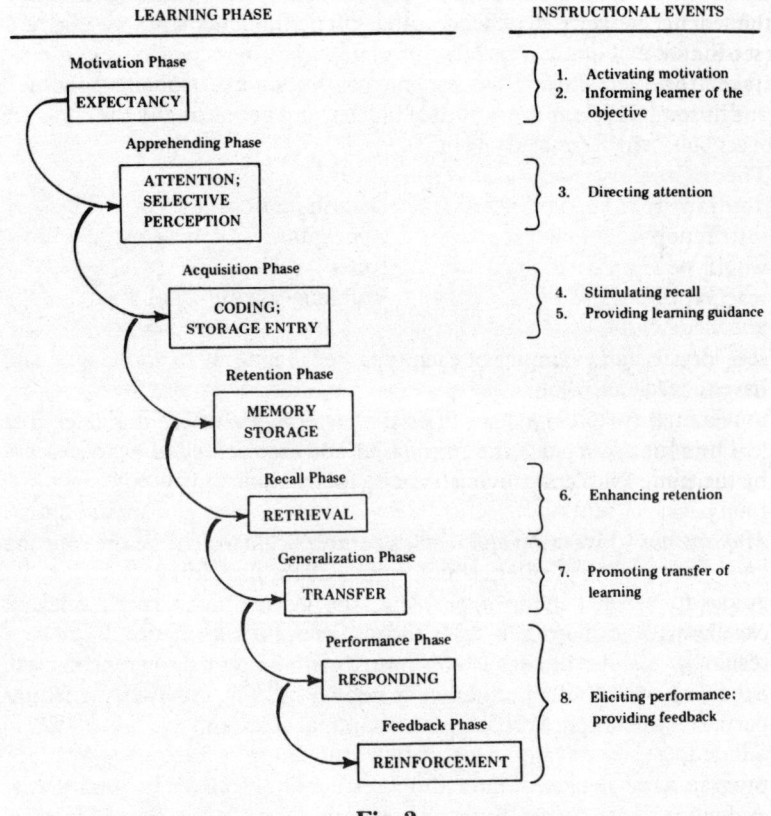

LEARNING PHASE	INSTRUCTIONAL EVENTS
Motivation Phase — EXPECTANCY	1. Activating motivation 2. Informing learner of the objective
Apprehending Phase — ATTENTION; SELECTIVE PERCEPTION	3. Directing attention
Acquisition Phase — CODING; STORAGE ENTRY	4. Stimulating recall 5. Providing learning guidance
Retention Phase — MEMORY STORAGE	
Recall Phase — RETRIEVAL	6. Enhancing retention
Generalization Phase — TRANSFER	7. Promoting transfer of learning
Performance Phase — RESPONDING	8. Eliciting performance; providing feedback
Feedback Phase — REINFORCEMENT	

Fig. 2.
Relation of the phases of learning to instructional events.

GAGNÉ, (1974) p. 119.

It is on the basis of these outcomes that he sets out principles for the planning of instruction. Knowledge can be translated into desired outcomes, and the necessary conditions and criteria for achievement specified. To some extent, there is a correspondence to Bruner's notions of predispositions, structure and sequence. Gagné's 'prerequisite learning' is a narrower concept than Bruner's 'predispositions', concentrating as it does solely on cognitive factors, and he is less interested in the internal logic of knowledge itself. 'Reinforcements', although again interpreted on the narrower basis of informational feedback, form part of Gagné's pedagogical principles.

ii) PEDAGOGY
From his basic model of learning and memory, Gagné derives a sequence of *learning phases* and the kinds of intervention ('instructional events') by the teacher which can help to ensure their successful accomplishment (see Figure 2).

Taken together, the analysis of learning outcomes and their conditions and 'instructional events' provide a comprehensive theory of instruction.

Theories of Instruction and Curriculum Planning
To draw up a curriculum in the light of Bruner's envisaged theory of instruction would be feasible only for large-scale curriculum projects. It would be quite unreasonable to expect any one school, let alone any one teacher, to possess the specialized and up-to-date expertise in areas of knowledge and cognitive processes that would be needed. Gagné, too, sees long-range curriculum planning as too big a job for those who also have to teach and would like to see 'a joint effort in schools and industry, universities and other agencies, working in consortium'.

The context, sequence, structure and materials would be worked out by the teams of experts, evaluated and perfected in field studies, and the final packages sent out to schools. Bruner's excursion into social studies, *Man a Course of Study* (MACOS) (see Bruner, 1966, Chs. 4 and 8) is a good example, with films, slides, tapes, written presentations, detailed guides for teachers and even a special training course for teachers. An excellent plan, one might think, constrained only by expense. But the results of such programmes have frequently been disappointing (see Schools Council, 1973) and it is perhaps naïve to attribute their only partial success to problems of dissemination or teacher bloody-mindedness. Two major American investigations of federal curriculum programmes suggest another interpretation. Both the eight-year evaluation of the *Follow Through* programme and the Rand Corporation's (1978) study of four other large-scale federal programmes, including *Right to Read*, found a lack of consistent success of individual programmes. All the curricula succeeded in some schools, but not in others, with no regular pattern of factors influencing success and failure. The Director of the Rand Corporation suggested that the model of education on which the programmes and their evaluation were based was mistaken — it is not a 'simple' matter of creating the perfect curriculum and persuading schools to adopt it; it might make for better learning to finance regions and schools to develop their own curricula in response to local conditions and needs. This expertly-designed, centrally-developed curriculum could perhaps be better seen as a flexible *resource,* rather than a foolproof blue print.

Bruner does not go so far as Gagné in adherence to a systems approach to curriculum planning. In Gagné and Briggs (1974, Ch. 11), the seductively rational steps in instructional system development are laid out (p. 213).

It is well to remember Stenhouse's (1975) caution about the application of systems theory to educational policies: 'It is concerned with efficiency, rather than with truth. That is not to be despised. But it should be noted that its concern with efficiency in the sense of value-for-investment provides an emphasis on *value* rather than *values.*' (my italics).

Objectives and Curriculum Planning
One of the major differences between the theories of Gagné and Bruner is in their use of objectives. Gagné's theory is firmly wedded to the classical model of behavioural objectives, while Bruner does not use the term.

The major argument for the objectives model is that clarity, efficiency and economy of effort are improved if we can specify exactly what we are trying to do and measure exactly how far we have succeeded. The main arguments against it are that trivial outcomes are the easiest to classify and measure and that close prespecification of objectives inhibits the teacher and learner from taking advantage of unexpected learning opportunities. Stenhouse (1975, Ch. 6) goes deeper. His fundamental criticisms of the objectives model, at least as a total pattern for education, are that it mistakes the nature of knowledge and that it mistakes the nature of the process of improving practice. He conceptualizes the processes of education as *training, instruction, initiation* and *induction* and sees the specification of objectives as helpful only in the first two. Gagné would disagree and argues that objectives for intellectual skills are not only possible but necessary.

It is difficult to make a rational assessment of theories of instruction and their relation to curriculum planning, as typified by Gagné, and very easy to be a 'true believer' or an 'unbeliever'. Stenhouse (1975) is surely right in saying: 'A systems approach rests on the foundation of objectives, but does not provide a method of defining such objectives'.

The values which inform what and how we teach are outside the scope of a theory of instruction. But given these values and an agreed context of knowledge, it is possible that a systematic approach, founded in the best available models of human learning and mental functioning, would sharpen our practice. Empirical trials in the classroom would show for which subjects, teachers and pupils it is appropriate.

FURTHER READING

J. S. Bruner, *Towards a Theory of Instruction*, 1966, is a readable introduction to the topic.

R. M. Gagné, *Essentials of Learning for Instruction*, 1974. A short book, setting out the essence of Gagné's theory of instruction, together with the learning model on which it is based.

QUESTIONS

1. To what extent and for which parts of your curriculum might Gagné's theory of instruction be useful?
2. How far do you consider Bruner's theory of instruction an adequate guide for curriculum planning? What additional information (if any) would you like?

14
Motivation and Curriculum Planning
Maggie Ing

Grand, over-arching theories of motivation can be seen as varying on at least two important dimensions:

    the basic biological _____ socially acquired pole,
                        and
    the internal pressures (innate or learned) _____ external stimuli pole

Their concepts, methods of enquiry and rigour in accepting 'evidence' also vary widely. The adoption of any one theory, psychological, psycho-analytic or behaviourist, is unlikely to provide satisfactory directives for education, because of the multiple nature of our aims and the complexity of the possible motives operating in schools. We are concerned with learning, not solely of a cognitive kind, within a social institution related to a network of other institutions, encompassing the untidy and blessed variety of human beings. Depending on what we are trying to do, it is possible to give an account of what happens in schools that emphasizes either the routine or the random, the universal or the unique. A reductionist account of human motives, however elegant as a theory, will not fit every case; yet there do seem to be patterns and regularities that make descriptive sense at some level.

At an intermediate level, between the over-arching and the individual, some concepts and parts of theories have been 'borrowed' by educational psychologists and translated into a loose set of prescriptions. These could be roughly classified as:

1. capitalizing on the presumed basic drive of curiosity, exploration, mastery of competence, as it has variously been labelled;
2. drawing upon hypothesized needs for 'ego-enhancement' or a good self-concept;
3. manipulating the consequences of actions to ensure desired patterns of learning;
4. arranging optimal presentation and cognitive feedback, on the assumption that knowing is its own reward.

As with other psychological theories, different models of curriculum tend to stress either the external-manipulative or internal-directed views of motivation.

Ausubel (1968) gives a typical set of maxims, mainly, though not exclusively, based on cognitive considerations, and largely agreed amongst psychologists.

1. Motivation can be an *effect* as well as a *cause* of learning.
2. The *goal* of learning should be made as explicit as possible.
3. Existing interests and motives should be used where possible, but they should not limit our efforts to promote learning.
4. Materials should stimulate intellectual curiosity.
5. Tasks should be appropriate to the learner, neither too difficult nor too easy.
6. Pupils should be helped to set their own goals, by the provision of good feedback.
7. We should take account of developmental and individual differences in motivation.
8. Rewards and punishments of an extrinsic kind should be sparingly and carefully used.

The teacher can hope to be sufficiently sensitive to his/her pupil's existing interests and motivations, but the planner of larger-scale curricula has obviously to depend on more generalized notions of the intended learners. The aspects of motivation within the scope of curriculum planning lie in the selection, presentation and organization of content, and in the provision of reinforcing feedback. Motivation involves two phases — the arousal of attention and interest, and the maintenance of willingness to learn. Initial attention can be a function of the perceptual qualities of the materials, movement, brightness, colour, so visual attractiveness and good audio-visual presentations are obviously desirable. Interest is a much more subjective and speculative concept. Attempts to devise curricula 'interesting' or 'relevant' to a particular wide group of learners are not always successful. Perhaps this is better done on a more local basis. The organization of what is to be learned, the demands made of the learner and the provision of feedback can help maintain motivation.

Programmed Instruction
Based on Skinner's operant conditioning, programmed instruction is one way of structuring learning units for which extravagant motivational claims have been made. Skinner originally thought that *active* responses by the learner at every step of the programme, high success rate brought

Motivation and Curriculum Planning

about by grading the steps so finely that error is almost impossible and the reinforcing effect of rewarding every correct response, were responsible for the demonstrably good learning on early automated instruction. Subsequent studies (e.g. Dale, 1967) have indicated that the breakdown of material to be learned into small parts (though Schramm, 1964, showed that sequence was not important at least with simple programmes), the provision of feedback and the opportunity to work at one's own pace are the likely factors in effective learning from programmes. Programmed instruction cannot deal with controverisal material, nor develop independent, critical thinking; but for the learning of straightforward information or skills, within the context of a wider course, it does seem to have motivational advantages.

Individualized Instruction

Only the *pace* of learning can be individual with programmed instruction; some indication of the variety of individualized instruction is given by Gagné and Briggs (1974) p. 187.

1. *Independent study plans,* in which there is agreement between a student and a teacher on only the most gross level of stating objectives to indicate the purpose of studying. The student works on his own to prepare for some form of final examination. No restrictions are placed upon the student as to how he may prepare for the examination. A course outline may or may not be provided. The task may be described at the course level in such terms as 'preparing for an examination in differential calculus,' or at the degree level as in 'honors programs' in English universities. A similar procedure in American practice is preparing for the doctoral comprehensive examination in psychology, English, or other named field.

2. *Self-directed study,* which may be undertaken with specific objectives agreed upon, but with no restriction upon how the student learns. Here the teacher may supply a list of objectives which define the test performances required to receive credit for the course; the teacher may also supply a list of readings or other resources available, but the student is not required to use them. If he passes the test, he receives credit for the course.

3. *Learner-centred programs,* in which the student decides a great deal for himself: within broadly defined areas what his objectives will be, how he will learn, and when he will decide to terminate one task and go to another. This degree of 'openness' is sometimes found in public schools, and has been the customary style of operation for a few private, special schools. Usually in public schools, learner choice is

permitted only for 'excursions' or 'enrichment' exercises, and then only after certain required or 'core' skills have been mastered. Often such excursions are offered as an incentive to the student to learn the core skills. This is an application of contingency management — offering a preferred activity contingent upon the prior mastery of a required activity.

4. *Self-pacing,* in which the learner works at his own rate, but upon objectives set by the teacher and required of all students. In this case all students may use the same materials to reach the same objectives — only the rate of progress is individualized.

5. *Student-determined instruction,* providing for student judgment in any or all of the following aspects of the learning: (a) selection of objectives; (b) selections of the particular materials, resources, or exercises to be used; (c) selection of a schedule within which work on different academic subjects will be allocated; (d) self-pacing in reaching each objective; (e) self-evaluation as to whether the objective has been met; and (f) freedom to abandon an objective in favor of another one. Obviously this description in itself implies the possibility of over twenty different ways in which instruction may be said to be 'individualized' or 'learner-determined'.

The central idea of an individualized, to some extent self-chosen, curriculum is nothing new to those familiar with good British primary schools. It obviously needs good resources, well-kept records and considerable powers of organization from the teacher.

The PLAN System
To those teachers who spend hours collecting and organizing resources, devising work-sheets and cards and struggling against time to attend to the progress of each of their pupils, the PLAN system described by Gagné and Briggs, 1974, may sound like their most delightful dreams.

PLAN is the basis of a curriculum (on a behavioural objectives model) in language, social studies, science and mathematics for grades 1-12. Within each grade and subject, the objectives are organized into modules of study for the students' use. The system is 'computer-supported' and a terminal, usually located in the school, receives and stores records of student progress, which can be printed out for the teacher.

The modules of study are composed of several teaching-learning units (TLUs) which begin with the objective, then direct the learner to what he is to do and finally provide him with self-test and discussion questions. Additional activities are set out in an accompanying Activity Sheet. On completion of these, the student takes a performance test. If he satisfies the computer, he goes on to the next TLU; if not, he does additional work under the teacher's guidance. Teacher directives accompany each TLU.

PLAN *could* be an imaginative use of technology to carry out desirable but difficult educational aims. However, the examples chosen by Gagné and Briggs, and presumably admired by them, do not seem superior to the ubiquitous duplicated worksheet which has not notably motivated pupils so far. 'Patriots and Politicians', a TLU in social studies for the seventh grade, for example, takes as its objective: Identify reasons for the development of political parties in the United States. It features an ill-drawn cartoon (with no joke that I can discern) presumably to orient the learner's attention and make him feel that it is an exciting task. Of the eight learning activities, five are reading—two or three pages at a time—from a textbook; one involves reading a newspaper; two invite discussion with a partner; and three looking at a filmstrip. The questions are mainly of a simple, factual type. Plainly, no technique is sufficient in itself to avoid pedestrian lessons. It is, of course, unrealistic to expect school life to be continuously engaging enthusiasm, but there is a difference between bread-and-butter learning within the context of enlarging curiosity and the same kind of practice and groundwork in the passive reception of what someone else thinks you ought to learn.

Discovery Learning
Bruner (1960) sees an element of 'discovery' in curricula as essential to developing the attitudes towards learning which are as important as the understanding of principles.

> Mastery of the fundamental ideas of a field involves not only the grasping of general principles, but also the development of an attitude toward learning and inquiry, toward guessing and hunches, toward the possibility of solving problems on one's own. Just what it takes to bring off such teaching is something on which a great deal of research is needed, but it would seem that an important ingredient is a sense of excitement about discovery—discovery of regularities of previously unrecognized relations and similarities between ideas, with a resulting sense of self-confidence in one's abilities.

Bruner gives the example of a sixth-grade class after conventional lessons on the social and economic geography of the South Eastern States of the USA, being asked to locate the major cities of the North Central region on a map without place names, but with only the physical features and natural resources indicated. The pupils had to think out and form hypotheses about the location of cities, something they had previously taken for granted, and the level of interest and depth of conceptualization they showed was above that of control groups taught by traditional means.

Ausubel (1968) doubts the *uniquely* motivating effect of 'discovery'. 'As every student who has been exposed to competent teaching knows, the skilful exposition of ideas can also generate considerable intellectual excitement and motivation for genuine inquiry, although admittedly not quite as much perhaps as does discovery.' Bruner claims that discovery-learning leads to more autonomous learning, freeing the child from dependence on extrinsic reinforcements like teacher and parent approval and good marks. Ausubel disagrees: 'there is no existing or necessary association between a discovery approach to learning and intrinsic motivation, on the one hand, and a reception approach to learning and extrinsic motivation on the other'. He links preferences for one or the other kind of motivation to the individual's need for self-esteem relative to cognitive needs in their own right.

In practice, it is relatively rare for anyone, child or not, to be *completely* self-motivated and since self-esteem can only develop through the esteem of others, the argument seems unnecessarily polarized. When Ausubel *reverses* Bruner's contention and says that discovery learning is more often associated with extrinsic motivation than is reception learning, it becomes absurd.

Mastery Learning
The principles, if not the implementation, of mastery learning are potentially a force for a radically different approach to curriculum planning and implementation. Enhanced motivation to learn would be only one effect. But if success is motivating to further effort (as it seems to be), it is possible that the expectation of success rather than failure would engage the endeavours of many pupils who are at present disaffected.

Bloom (1976) starts firmly from the assumption that most people are capable of learning most tasks in school: '... very few learning tasks provided in the schools require neurological or other capabilities which exceed that potentially available to most humans'. Yet, according to Block (1971) 'the schools continue to provide successful and rewarding learning experiences for only about one-third of our learners'. Block continues: 'Theoretically, therefore, by breaking a complex behaviour down into a chain of component behaviours and by ensuring student mastery of each link in the chain, it would be possible for any student to master even the most complex skills'.

Bloom *et al.*, 1971, dismiss the accepted normal distribution of school achievement: 'There is nothing sacred about the normal curve. It is the distribution most appropriate to chance and random activity... If we are

Motivation and Curriculum Planning

effective in our instruction, the distribution of achievement should be very different from the normal curve'.

Carroll (1963) had previously defined aptitude as the time taken to learn a task under ideal instructional conditions. Bloom (1976) has translated Carroll's earlier scheme into a working model:

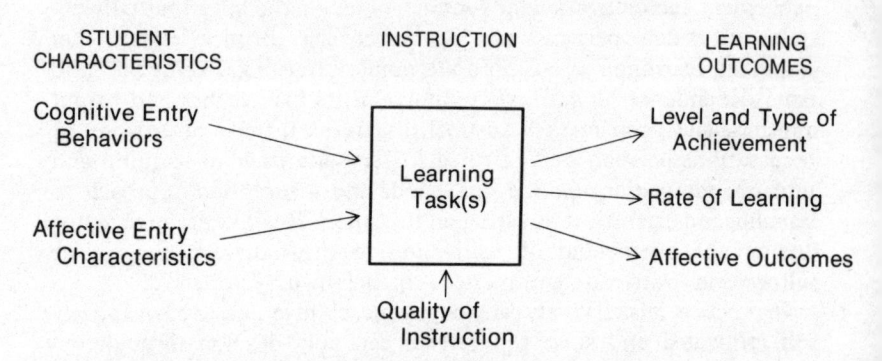

```
STUDENT              INSTRUCTION           LEARNING
CHARACTERISTICS                            OUTCOMES

Cognitive Entry                            Level and Type of
Behaviors          ┌──────────┐            Achievement
         ────────→ │ Learning │ ────────→
                   │ Task(s)  │ ────────→  Rate of Learning
Affective Entry    │          │ ────────→
Characteristics    └──────────┘            Affective Outcomes
         ────────→      ↑
                   Quality of
                   Instruction
```

MAJOR VARIABLES IN THE THEORY OF SCHOOL LEARNING

If the cognitive and affective (motivational in this context) entry behaviour of the student can be specified and the quality of instruction suited to his needs, then learning outcomes will be favourable. Bloom sets out to explain the variables and to examine the ways in which they can be altered to improve learning *in relation to particular tasks*.

The vision of schools which *expect* success from 90-95 per cent of their pupils, which concern themselves with the development of talent and not merely the selection of talent, is stirring, if not entirely new. But some of Bloom's statements about individual differences are questionable.

After almost a decade of work on mastery learning and research on some of the variables involved in mastery learning, we have come to the conclusion that individual differences in school learning under very favourable conditions will approach a vanishing point while under the least favourable conditions they will be greatly exaggerated.

A vanishing point? This suggests either a very restricted notion of school learning, or a naïvete about the operation of individual differences.

The main thesis of this book is that *individual differences in learning* is an observable phenomenon which can be predicted, explained and altered in a great variety of ways. In contract, *individual differences in learners* is a more esoteric notion. It frequently obscures our efforts to deal directly with educational problems in that it searches for explanations in the person of the learner rather than in the *interaction* between individuals and the educational and social environments in which they have been placed.

This is undoubtedly true, but not at all the same as claiming that a system which provided each learner with the time, and type and quality of instruction best suited to him would eliminate differences in achievement.

Bloom (1976) provides evidence for the improvement of learning when corrective feedback is given after each learning task. Unfortunately, he does not tell us how many learners were in his groups, nor how similar or dissimilar they were in their 'Cognitive Entry Behaviours'.

Like Gagné, he seems to assume that specifying the prerequisite learning for specific tasks is relatively simple. I suggest that this is true only for simple tasks, and for relatively homogeneous learners.

Block (1971) comments: 'Typically past mastery learning strategies have been implemented in single subjects. The greatest pay-off in terms of student development, however, is likely to result from the implementation of an entire mastery curriculum'.

Bloom admits that the theory deals with specific tasks. We may well question whether it could be implemented over an entire school curriculum—it would be unrealistic to expect some students to fit in the extra time they would need during out-of-school hours, and those who needed less time would inevitably go beyond minimal competence, or learn more things, or endure greater boredom.

We could undoubtedly improve our techniques of instruction (though not from reading Bloom, who suggests little by way of teaching strategies) and give better feedback to our pupils; by making possible greater success for a greater number, we could undoubtedly improve motivation.

But *what* is it that our students are to learn? Stenhouse (1978) in reviewing Bloom found the book 'explicitly optimistic, implicitly pessimistic about the possible results of schools'. True, Bloom says, 'the theory does not deal with the underlying values of the education enterprise'. Perhaps it is this avoidance of values from which limited and sterile values seem to emerge, especially in the examples of learning tasks, which inclines me to agree with Stenhouse that Bloom's notion of 'mastery learning' is much closer to 'minimal learning'.

The association of Mastery Learning with a strictly behavioural objectives model of curriculum is unnecessarily limiting. There are undoubtedly advantages, motivational as well as organizational, in defining what should be achieved at the end of a course; but to insist on specifying *every* outcome is unrealistic; even worse is to accept as valid *only* those outcomes which can be defined in behavioural terms, which is to adopt an operational definition of learning. Sockett (1973) succinctly points out the inherent flaws in this approach. Motivation to learn in school is usually determined in many ways. An eclectic approach, like that suggested by Ausubel, is likely to be more fruitful than adherence to any one, over-simplified theory.

FURTHER READING

B. S. Bloom, J. T. Hastings and G. Madaus, *Handbook on Formative and Summative Evaluation of Student Learning*, 1971, Ch. 3. A summary of 'mastery learning' theory.

L. Stenhouse, 'School Mastery', *Times Educational Supplement*, 6 January 1978. A brief, trenchant attack on Bloom's position.

C. R. Rogers, *Freedom to Learn*, 1969. A very different view of motivation as essentially personal. Highly readable, in the romantic tradition.

QUESTIONS

1. To what extent do you agree that motivation is the job of the individual teacher and cannot be built in to a curriculum plan?
2. Discuss 'mastery learning' in relation to the notion that all pupils should achieve at least minimal competence in the most important areas of the curriculum.

15
Curriculum Evaluation
Denis Lawton

Introduction
For many years evaluation has been the most neglected aspect of curriculum studies. Evaluation has been seen in a very limited way as measuring the success of teaching in terms of pupils' learning. More fundamental questions about the value of the learning programme have often been ignored. This should not surprise us: if curriculum studies is a very difficult aspect of educational theory, it is also the case that questions of evaluation present some of the most difficult problems in curriculum studies. Evaluation is not simply concerned with how well students have learnt something, but also with questions of justification and the unintended consequences of learning.

In England, curriculum evaluation developed largely as a by-product of various curriculum development projects. Those who had financed the innovation sometimes wanted to know whether it was working. But evaluation is always political in some sense: it is political in the sense of implying some kind of control; and it is political in the sense that some particular kinds of evaluation have the effect (intentional or unintentional) of keeping teachers down to a more humble role than they would like. 'Evaluation is always derived from biased origins. When someone wants to defend something or to attack something, he often evaluates it' (House, 1973, p. 3).

Definitions of Evaluation
One difficulty in defining evaluation is that the word is used in a variety of ways with imprecise or overlapping meanings. Evaluation is much wider than measurement. Although it does not necessarily exclude the use of assessment or measuring techniques, it does direct attention to other aspects of the learning process and its context. Evaluation is concerned more fundamentally with deciding on the value or 'worthwhileness' of a learning process as well as the effectiveness with which it is being carried out. For example, it is fairly easy to *measure* a child's achievement in memorizing the capes and bays of the British Isles,

Curriculum Evaluation

and express the performance in terms of a single percentage; an *evaluation* might however come to the conclusion that such learning was completely without educational value.

Measurement is also usually (but not necessarily) concerned with results over a short period, whereas educationists ought to be concerned with long-term effects; history teachers test what pupils have remembered at the end of a term or year; this is important, but even more crucial is whether pupils would be reading history books or applying their knowledge 20 years later. It would be impracticable to attempt that kind of measurement, but an evaluator might make reasonable assumptions about the kind of history teaching which will produce short-term memorization without long-term understanding, enjoyment or application. But some assumptions are more reasonable than others — some look suspiciously like personal preference or bias.

If evaluation tends to be biased because evaluators usually have an axe to grind (consciously or unconsciously) it may also be important to be aware of different structural models of evaluations so that other kinds of control may be detected and guarded against. A naïve view of evaluation is that a neutral evaluator applies certain objective standards to an educational programme, and then produces some kind of evaluation answer, preferably in the form of neat percentages. The reality is much more complex. An evaluator will use (whether consciously or not) a model of some kind which will have certain in-built assumptions, advantages and disadvantages. Five models will be examined in this chapter, but it should be noted that these are overlapping models and it is unlikely that any one evaluation would fit neatly into a single model.

1. The Classical Experimental Model

Educationists as diverse as Bobbitt (1918) and Hirst (1965) have suggested that planning requires the specification of clear objectives. Perhaps the clearest statement of this policy is in Tyler's book (1949). Tyler, as mentioned in Ch. 10, suggested four fundamental questions which he thought must be answered in connection with any curriculum:

1. What educational purposes should the school seek to obtain?
2. What educational experiences can be provided that are likely to attain these purposes?
3. How can these educational experiences be effectively organized?
4. How can we determine whether these purposes are being attained?

These four principal questions have been translated into an even simpler model: objectives — content — organization and method — evaluation. If evaluation shows that specified objectives have not been attained it must mean that the content chosen or the methods of teaching and organization used were not appropriate. This model has the virtue of great simplicity and the attraction that it makes possible the transformation of education into a 'scientific' process. Since Tyler the model has developed in at least two ways: first, the refinement of the meaning of objectives and, secondly, the elaboration of the four stage model into more sophisticated versions.

It soon became clear that an objective meant different things to different people. Eventually the only acceptable kind of objectives became behavioural objectives—that is, pre-specified changes in pupil behaviour which could be measured. To express objectives in terms of teacher behaviour or class reactions which could not be measured was unacceptable.

Another kind of clarification which was explored in the late 1940s and early 1950s was associated with Bloom. In 1948 there was a meeting in Boston of university examiners. During the course of discussion these educationists, many of whom were psychologists specializing in psychometrics, became more and more aware that there was a good deal of confusion regarding objectives, methods and the terminology surrounding the curriculum and examinations that they were involved in. They decided to work on a system of classifying objectives, which was later published as *The Taxonomy of Educational Objectives*, (1956) edited by Bloom and some of his colleagues.

Bloom began postulating three domains of educational objectives: the cognitive or intellectual domain, the affective or emotional domain, and the psychomotor domain which was concerned with physical skills. The original intention was to provide a taxonomy (or system of classification arranged hierarchically) of objectives in terms of measured changes in student behaviour. These were arranged from the simplest kinds of learning, at the top of the list, to the most complex at the bottom. Knowledge of specific facts is regarded as much more simple than the understanding of abstraction, and the most complex of understanding is the judgment or evaluation of theories and evidence. A number of criticisms have been made of Bloom's taxonomy and he certainly does not regard it as entirely acceptable himself any longer. One of these criticisms is that it is not satisfactory to separate knowledge into the three domains. Some feel that more is lost that is gained by such an analysis.

A second criticism concerns the taxonomy itself; while recognizing the value of emphasizing that there are important aspects of learning to be assessed other than those which are most easily examined (such as items of information easily memorized), evaluation is necessary throughout the taxonomy and it may be a little misleading to leave evaluation until the end.

Curriculum Evaluation

Another objection concerns the emphasis on behavioural objectives. It is probably axiomatic that teachers should be as clear as they can be about what it is that they are trying to do in the classroom, but to suggest that this might amount to expressing the whole of the teacher-pupil relationship in terms of pre-specified objectives is a very different question. There are philosophical as well as practical arguments which suggest that the objectives point of view in curriculum planning, and therefore the objectives model in curriculum evaluation, will simply not stand close scrutiny. It might be possible to pre-specify behavioural objectives in the early teaching of reading skills, but Lawrence Stenhouse (1970) has pointed out the difficulty of pre-specifying behavioural objectives in such areas as the study of literature. How many teachers would claim to understand Shakespeare well enough to specify objectives in a lesson on *Hamlet*, for example?

Another of the problems of the Tyler-Bloom model is that it takes objectives for granted when they might be highly contentious. We need to know where the objectives come from. A more deep-rooted objection is that the model is related to a rather inhuman, behaviourist view of life as well as to the least attractive aspects of modern industrialist society. Those who dislike this model of curriculum refer to it as the industrial or even the factory model of curriculum. The corresponding model of evaluation is sometimes also referred to as the agricultural or botanical model. Such terminology is used as an implicit criticism of the classical educational experiment which treated learning as a simple matter and regarded evaluation as a process of:

    a) pre-testing;
    b) administering the teaching programme;
    c) post-testing;
    d) comparing results with a control group which had not had the teaching programme

just as an agricultural experiment would test the efficiency of a fertilizer by

    a) measuring the height of the plant; then
    b) applying the fertilizer;
    c) measuring the plant again, and
    d) comparing the growth with that of plants in a control group without the fertilizer.

Much of the reaction against applying that kind of simple experimental design to children's learning is that the teaching- learning situation in human beings is very complex. For example, human beings perform differently when under observation— cabbages do not; the unintended consequences of human influence are likely to be much more important in any situation involving human beings. For these reasons, evaluators have sought alternative approaches to the complex problem of curriculum evaluation.

2. The Illuminative or Social Anthropological Paradigm

Alternative models of evaluation have developed partly to meet objections to the classical models but also for more positive reasons. Parlett and Hamilton produced a paper in 1972 which was extremely important, 'Evaluation as Illumination'. Much of the interest in the new kind of evaluation is that it shifts the style of educational research generally, as well as curriculum evaluation in particular, away from a narrow psychological view of human behaviour to a much more social anthropological view.

Another motive for change was the comparative lack of success or failure of 'take-up' of many large and expensive curriculum projects in both the USA and the UK. It was found that teachers, when they were free to make a choice, appeared to be highly resistant to the apparent advantages of particular curriculum programmes even when there was 'evidence' to show that the reformed programmes were better than the traditional alternatives. The Schools Council's recent 'Impact and Take-up' Project throws additional light on this problem. Another aspect of the classical experimental model which began to be criticized was the emphasis on size: a necessary feature of traditional experiments was that large samples were necessary to indicate differences that could be measured and seen to be statistically significant. However, many evaluators came to the conclusion that large samples were not only unnecessary and costly, but might have even more important disadvantages. Robert Stake, for example, suggested that what was needed, at this stage, was a panoramic viewfinder rather than a microscope. This was not intended as a criticism of all empirical methods, but was simply asserting that evaluators had moved towards detailed measurement much too soon; they should have first acquired a better means of describing the whole picture of the situation they were trying to evaluate.

In December 1972, a conference of the 'new wave' evaluators was held at Cambridge. The participants were not in agreement on all issues, but they published a statement which indicated some major shifts in concern. They suggested:

1. that traditional methods of evaluation had paid too little attention to the whole education processes in a particular milieu, and too much attention to those changes in student behaviour which could be measured;
2. that the educational research climate had under-estimated the gap

between school problems and conventional research issues;
3. that curriculum evaluation should be responsive to the requirements of different audiences, illuminative of complex organizational processes, and relevant to both public and professional decisions about education.
MACDONALD AND PARLETT (1973, pp. 79-80).

A number of criticisms have been made about the illuminative model of evaluation: first, although there are established rules of procedure for anthropologists working in primitive societies, and participant observers working within organizations, these procedures are controversial, and it does not necessarily follow that they can be carried over into evaluation or educational case studies. Second, the rules of procedure for non-traditional evaluation are insuffuciently clear, and the skills (both professional and personal) needed by evaluators should be specified more clearly. There is as yet no tradition comparable to the established standards in historical and social research. Third, there is a danger of personal, subjective impressions being put forward as objective data. Fourth, the problem of role conflict is enormous for evaluators and may place them under conditions of considerable strain. Fifth, there is a danger that because of these difficulties evaluators will develop esoteric methods and language which will make curriculum evaluation just as remote from teachers and administrators as conventional educational research.

3. The Briefing Decision-Makers Model
MacDonald (1973) has suggested that curriculum evaluation is concerned with providing information for decision-makers. He extends this concept (1976) to include the essentially political nature of curriculum evaluation. Evaluation is inevitably concerned with attitudes to the distribution of power in educational control and curricula control in particular. Outlining three ideal types of bureaucratic, autocratic and democratic evaluation, MacDonald suggests that the style of an evaluation is related to a particular 'political stance'. He maintains that much research, including educational research, is related to ideology. Evaluators should stop pretending that they are value-free and be more explicit about what the values under discussion are. For MacDonald, evaluation is clearly not a simple matter of making a judgment about the value of an educational programme and then passing it on to the decision-makers; it is a complex process of collecting information (including judgments) which will enable the decision-makers to make a more rational choice. The evaluator is also concerned with making judgments, but he should realize that the final choice is not necessarily

his. This does not mean that the evaluator is simply concerned with passing on information which the decision-makers will find acceptable; it does mean that the evaluator has to recognize the value stance of the decision-makers. The evaluator has to be aware of the total context of the educational programme.

Against this general background of evaluation for decision-making, MacDonald describes his three 'ideal types'. The implication is that evaluators ought to find out what type of evaluation they are getting involved in and negotiate a contract accordingly (or perhaps decide not to):

1. Bureaucratic evaluation is an unconditional service to those government agencies which have major control over the allocation of educational resources. The evaluator accepts the values of those who hold office, and offers information which will help to accomplish their policy objectives. He acts as a management consultant.
2. Autocratic evaluation is a conditional service; it offers external validation of policy in exchange for compliance with its recommendations; the evaluator focuses upon issues of educational merit, and acts as expert adviser.
3. Democratic evaluation is an information service to the whole community about the characteristic of an educational programme; a democratic evaluator recognizes value pluralism and seeks to represent a range of interest in his issue formulation; the evaluator acts as a broker in exchanges of information between groups who want knowledge of each other. His techniques of data gathering and representation must be accessible to non-specialist audiences. The report is non-recommendatory.

MACDONALD in TAWNEY (1976, pp. 133-4).

While the three styles are unlikely to exist in a pure form, in any evaluation study one style is likely to predominate.

In the USA the bureaucratic style of evaluation still dominates the scene despite some vigorous criticisms. In 1973, 13 states had passed legislation which related teacher tenure to the achievement of performance-based objectives (which were predetermined by administrators and merely assessed by evaluators). The long-term effects of such evaluation are increased power and control by the administrative decision-makers. Autocratic evaluation also has an interesting history in the USA. Experts are hired to make decisions about the relative merits of various curriculum programmes, and by this method the administrators effectively get what they want without taking the blame for the ultimate decision.

Democratic evaluation is in an early stage of development. In the USA, Robert Stake has advocated that evaluators be responsive to a range of different audiences and interests. Stake suggests more openness in evaluation to reflect pluralist values. Rather than make recommendations, the evaluator should make public the nature of the problems of a range of issues, decisions on which would have to be taken by informed citizenry. In the UK the Ford Safari project, directed by Barry MacDonald, is exploring the democratic model in a study of the effects of a number of curriculum development projects.

4. The Teacher as Researcher Model

The conventional view of the teacher in a good deal of the early literature on curriculum development (especially the classical model) was that the teacher was a kind of technician who, having certain skills of knowledge transmission, could easily be persuaded to change both the content of what was to be transmitted and the method of transmission, if only a curriculum developer could get the message across to him. A good deal of early curriculum development in the USA and elsewhere was based on this assumption. The central team formulated objectives, put together material which would be suitable content: made recommendations for the organization and methods of teaching, and handed this package over to the teachers, and eventually all this was evaluated. The teacher, according to the model, was an unfortunate but necessary intermediary between the mind of the curriculum planner and a larger number of pupils. The reality is very different. A teacher is not a passive transmitter of other people's ideas; all teachers transform material in the process of their teaching. There is no such thing as teacher-proof materials.

Secondly, no two schools and no two classes are sufficiently alike to allow for this kind of mass production of curriculum change. There are too many variables to make possible the neat controlled experiment which was discussed and criticized above under the classical experimental model. The teacher should be recognized as a key figure in any kind of curriculum change: it is impossible to do without him, and foolish to ignore him. One way of acknowledging the central role of the teacher in curriculum development is to regard him as a professional who looks upon his own teaching as research rather than as a routine process of knowledge transmission.

The major exponent of this view of the teacher as researcher is Stenhouse (1975). He does not accept the distinction between curriculum evaluation and curriculum development, and finds it an advantage to cast the teacher researcher not 'in the role of the creator or man with a mission, but in that of the investigator. The curriculum he creates is then to be judged by whether it advances our knowledge rather than by whether it is right. It is conceived as a probe through which to explore and test hypotheses and not as a recommendation to be accepted' (p. 125). Stenhouse illustrates his suggestions by reference to his own research into teaching about race relations.

John Elliott was formerly a member of the Humanities Curriculum Project and an associate of Lawrence Stenhouse. He is now Director of the Ford Teaching Project based at the Cambridge Institute. The project developed from Stenhouse's ideas and Elliott's conviction that the curriculum reform movement had almost entirely failed at the level of classroom implementation. Elliott has suggested that reformers failed to realize that fundamental changes in classroom practice can only be carried out if teachers become conscious of the theories which guide that practice and are able to reflect critically on those theories. Elliott felt that many of the problems in the HCP discussion-based enquiry approaches were caused by teachers' 'habitual and unconscious behaviour patterns'.

The Ford Teaching Project started with 40 teachers who were supported by a central team of two researchers and a secretary. In addition, two local authority advisers helped on a part-time basis. The problem to be investigated was concerned with the dissonance between practice and aspirations of a group of teachers implementing enquiry and discovery approaches. The methods of data collection included the teachers keeping field notes, and pupils keeping diaries which enabled teachers to monitor their own performance, and to begin to perceive problems more carefully as a first stage towards solutions. This concept of self-monitoring was a crucial one, and Elliott and his colleague, Adelman, make a distinction between:

1. teachers who are adopting an objective stance to their practice, but require support in collecting and analyzing more sufficient data as a basis for constructing accurate accounts.
2. teachers who are not adopting an objective stance but in as much as they sense or feel a situation to be problematic are ready to do so.
3. teachers who are neither ready nor able to adopt an objective stance to their practice.

ELLIOTT and ADELMAN, Unit 28 of Open University Course E203 (1975)

It soon became apparent that the majority of teachers had difficulty in monitoring their own practice. It was necessary to develop strategies that would motivate teachers, so Elliott and Adelman decided on a more interventionist approach which they called 'triangulation'.

The idea of triangulation is derived from Cicourel. It relies on the intervention of an outsider to produce certain social effects:

Curriculum Evaluation

Triangulation involves gathering accounts of a teaching situation from three quite different points of view; namely, those of a teacher, his pupils and a participant observer. Who in the triangle gathers the accounts, how they are elicited, who compares them, depends largely on the context. The process of gathering accounts from three distinct stand-points has an epistemological justification. Each point of the triangle stands in a unique epistemological position with respect to access to relevant data about a teaching situation. The teacher is in the best position to gain access via introspection to his own intentions and aims in the situation. The students are in the best position to explain how the teachers' actions influence the way they respond to the situation. The participant observer is in the best position to collect data about the observable features of the interactions between teachers and pupils. By comparing his own accounts with accounts from the other two stand-points a person at one point in the triangle has an opportunity to test and perhaps revise it on the basis of more sufficient data.

ibid., p. 74.

Triangulation methods have proved to be an excellent way of encouraging self-monitoring practices by teachers, and also a means of promoting discussion and classification by teachers who would wish to be involved at that stage in triangulation studies both of a personality and a technical nature which have yet to be completely solved.

5. The Case Study Model in Evaluation

Most of the non-traditional methods of evaluation so far discussed have involved some use of case studies. Unfortunately, this is a term which has a wide variety of meanings inside and outside education. A case study is an analytical or descriptive study of a single event, organization or programme in appropriate detail: this might take the form of a description of a school undergoing change, or one class, or even a single lesson. In the past, case studies have been regarded with some suspicion by curriculum evaluators who favour the 'hard data' of test scores etc., but as we have seen, such data is by no means as good as is sometimes assumed, and even when it is good, it may need to be supplemented by the kind of detail which can only be provided by informed description.

In December 1975 a second conference was held at Cambridge to define new approaches. In a Report, *Rethinking Case Study*, written by Adelman, Jenkins and Kemmis, the advantages of case studies were summarized. They also spelt out three 'aspirations':

1. demystification (setting out more clearly the methodology, rules for

interviews, observation, data control and processing, as well as presentation of the data);
2. a code of practice for evaluators especially regarding the rights of those being studied (the ethic of case study);
3. plans for a handbook of principles, procedures and methods for case study work in education.

In establishing these principles of procedure and practice, the evaluators had two main traditions to guide their developing methodology: historical research and the established tradition of social anthropology. It should be stressed, however, that a case study in education is in many respects very different from either a historical study or work on a non-industrial society. A case study is also very different from participant observation, although some of the rules which have been developed for participant observation may be useful as a rough guide later to be fashioned into more precise rules.

As a very crude generalization, it might be true to see a certain affinity between the objectives approach of the experimental model and behaviourist psychology, whereas non-traditional evaluation is closer to techniques of history and anthropology. However, this separation should not be exaggerated and it certainly must not be assumed that the two models are incompatible. It is possible to be eclectic, and the art of evaluation is partly a matter of knowing the strengths and weaknesses of a wide range of techniques, and also knowing when one particular technique would have sufficient advantage to outweight its disadvantages.

FURTHER READING
Beyond the Numbers Game, 1977, edited by David Hamilton, David Jenkins, Christine King, Barry MacDonald and Malcolm Parlett, is a very useful collectiion of papers about non-traditional evaluation.
David Tawney's collection of Schools Council evaluation studies is a good review of the practical application of various methods, *Curriculum Evaluation Today: Trends and Implications,* 1976.

QUESTIONS
1. Why is the 'classical model' of evaluation now regarded as inadequate?
2. What to you understand by 'illuminative evaluation'?
3. Draw up a list of rules for case study as a method of evaluation.

Conclusion
Peter Gordon

It will have been seen throughout this book that many questions relating to the curriculum have been posed in recent years. At a time of shrinking resources and falling rolls, schools are likely to be asked to justify their activities in more detail than was formerly the case. Also, in an increasingly technological society, the relationship or 'match' between school curriculum and the needs of future adults is being questioned. What used to be accepted as a four or five year course of instruction in secondary schools which could be tested by means of conventional examination must now take account of different forms of evaluation and attempts to assess a much wider range of pupils than was formerly the case. The process of decision-making, or who gets what, is no longer the sole province of individual departments or teachers. Newer teaching techniques and a re-evaluation of the nature of knowledge, as represented in the different disciplines, have had an effect on curriculum planning. The change to comprehensive schooling, often involving increased size of units, has led to discussion on appropriate forms of school organization to ensure curriculum co-ordination. Not least important are the increasingly interventionist role by central government in curriculum matters and the general politicization of the curriculum on a number of issues. No realistic study of the curriculum therefore would be complete without attempting to ascertain how these and other factors are likely to affect the way in which schools operate.

The Relationship between the Central Authority, Local Education Authorities and Schools
At the central level, it would no longer be entirely true, to quote from a recent Permanent Under Secretary to the Department of Education, to state that 'the Department's role in relation to the school curriculum has traditionally been strictly limited' (Pile, 1979, p. 94). The Report on the Circular 14/77 review of local authority curricular arrangements, published in 1979, emphasized that the promotion of education

> must involve an overall view of the content and quality of education seen from the standpoint of national policies and needs as well as the

Conclusion

resources devoted to it. The Secretaries of State do not seek to determine in detail what the schools should teach or how it should be taught; but they have an inescapable duty to satisfy themselves that the work of the schools matches national needs.
DES, *Local Authority Arrangements for the School Curriculum,* 1979, p.2.

The document issued by the Secretary of State, *A Framework for the School Curriculum,* (1980) spells out the key elements in a curriculum which every pupil should experience during his or her period of education. There is in the document a clear indication to local authorities and schools that responsibility for curriculum policy must be taken more seriously. On the part of local authorities, this is likely to lead to more curricular supervision, ensuring that resources are deployed to meet curriculum needs: schools should provide relevant information for monitoring to the local authority.

Whilst such suggestions are a sensible step forward, there are potential difficulties in their implementation. The somewhat naïve statement made in the *Framework* document (p. 2) that 'schools are likely to be more effective in achieving their curricular aims if these aims are clearly set out in writing', leaves out of account other very important factors. It has been argued by John Tomlinson (1979), Director of Education for Cheshire and Chairman of the Schools Council, that local education authorities need to be able to plan their policies further ahead than is possible under the present yearly budgeting system. This has become increasingly necessary considering, for example, that primary schools will be a third smaller by 1984, and that 70 per cent of the schools will have to organize classes with mixed age groups, and teachers who have never done so before will have to teach them. If a coherent policy of curriculum thinking, in-service training and resource distribution is to be formulated, longer term planning is essential.

Another important aspect of the new relationship between the Department of Education and Science, local authorities and the schools in curriculum matters is the type of accountability procedures to be adopted. Much depends however, as was pointed out in Chapter 8, on the form which accountability may take. The document *Education in Schools* (1977), mentioned some of the dangers of centrally imposed testing procedures. These include the risk of distorting the curriculum by coaching for tests and thus possibly lowering rather than raising standards and the informal or formal establishment of 'league tables' of school performance based on test results which do not take into account differences between school catchment areas. The Report hoped that 'increasingly schools should assess their own performance against their

Conclusion

own objectives as well as external criteria' (p. 17). How far the monitoring procedures of achievement of children at school by the Assessment of Performance Unit can avoid such dangers remains to be seen. It would be unfortunate if there was official encouragement of the policy of some local authorities, as reported in the DES Report on Education *Assessing the Performance of Pupils* (1978, p.3), in mounting their own monitoring surveys using test material from a variety of sources. The matter is placed in its proper perspective in the HMI statement *A View of the Curriculum* (1980) when it mentions the need for mutual confidence between schools and the wider public in agreement on aims and how they may be realized.

> In practice that means that the broad definition of the purposes of school education is a shared responsibility, whereas the detailed means by which this may best be realized in individual schools and for individual children are a matter for professional judgement.
> (pp. 2-3)

Examinations and the Curriculum

At the secondary level especially, account must be taken of the relationship between curriculum and examinations. A constant complaint of teachers has been that both desirable teaching methods and content were subordinated to the prime need of externally imposed examination syllabuses. The Waddell Committee appointed by the Secretary of State in 1976 to consider proposals for replacing the General Certificate of Education Ordinary Level and the Certificate of Secondary Education by a common system of examining, made clear that it wholly accepted the principle that the curriculum should lead (1978, Part I, p. 8). The development of a scheme for a common system of examining which would involve teachers more centrally in matters of curriculum and assessment provides an opportunity to identify subject 'cores' common to a wide range of pupils' ability. (See the deliberations of the Educational Study Group of the Waddell Committee, 1978, Vol. II, pp. 7-76.) The new 16 plus examination announced by the Government in February 1980, envisaging a reduction in the number of different syllabuses which can be offered for any particular subject, is a step in the right direction.

A more conscious attempt to determine a core curriculum derives from the Keohane Committee set up in 1978 to consider an examination for sixth formers staying on for only one year. It recommended (1979, p. 33), with a view to preparing young people effectively for employment, that the desirable basic elements of the course should include improving competence in basic communication and numerical skills, as well as vocationally-oriented studies.

Conclusion

These interesting attempts to relate curriculum and examinations fail to take account of the sizeable proportion of pupils who do not take any public examinations at 16: nor do they include the total six-form school population, especially those staying on until 18. The still patchy system of examination therefore presents difficulties to those wishing to design curricular programmes in broader terms.

Schools as Sources of Curriculum Renewal
So far in this conclusion, we have been considering some of the determinants of curriculum which are external to schools. How far can schools, as independent entities, develop their programmes? King and Brownell (1966) placed prime importance on the need for schools to have a system of governance which is consistent with their own essential character (p. 169). One of the ways in which this may be achieved is for teachers to fully participate, or have means of representation in policy-making bodies. The hierarchical nature of authority in schools does not easily accommodate forums for discussion on curriculum. It seems strange that there is no equivalent in schools of the Weaver-type statutory bodies found in colleges and in further education, where members of staff can take part in discussion on a range of professional issues, not least those which pertain to curriculum. Suggestions put forward by Richardson (1973, 1975) provide some basis for ways in which staffs could deliberate on curriculum matters. The patterns of school organization, mentioned in Chapter 9, presuppose a wider involvement of staff than exists at present.

Such changes in the nature of decision-making in the curriculum in schools (and this also assumes that other bodies in the community are represented as well) have implications for the professional standing of teachers. There will be a need for greater competence and knowledge of assessment techniques which refer to the qualitative as well as the more traditional quantifiable aspects. More expertise is required in handling different forms of inquiry, of organizing instruction around constant threads or elements, concepts, skills or values (Goodlad, 1966, p. 240). Equally, the teacher should be able to judge the appropriateness or otherwise of employing criterion-referenced programmes in classrooms (Rutherford, 1979). Greater understanding of classroom processes is also essential. Barnes has pointed out that an effective curriculum is shaped just as much by pupils' 'objectives', beliefs and values as by those of the teacher. 'A psychological model of learning is not enough: for curriculum theory a social model is needed, for it must acknowlege both learner and social milieu and include communication from pupil to teacher as well as *vice versa.*'(Barnes, 1976, p. 188).

The implications of such a programme of in-service training are far

Conclusion

reaching, as Tomlinson (1979) argued:

> ...if curriculum is to be simplified and agreed, if examinations are to be unified and their competence to judge what is being taught extended appropriately, our teachers must be given the time to learn these things, time to think how they should be used in their schools, and time to apply them.

Finally, it is important that some attention should be paid to the present state of curriculum theory. As was shown in Chapter 10, the different models put forward by writers are, for the most part, either based on a belief in behavioural objectives or a reaction from them. The rational planning model, as stated by Tyler and Popham in the USA and by Hirst in England (though the latter does not claim that all objectives need necessarily be expressed in behavioural terms) has been widely criticized on many grounds (Taylor and Richards, 1979, pp. 69-71). On the other hand, the views of Stenhouse and Eisner which argue against prespecifying in advance the nature of pupils' responses, especially in the literary, fine arts and aesthetic fields, present difficulties in an era of accountability. Attempts to accommodate theory and practice together have resulted in a number of interesting formulations, such as those of Skilbeck and Lawton, which take into account the cultural framework, the political context of curriculum making and changes in ideology. There is, in the present day climate, the need for middle ground theory which will satisfy the differing viewpoints of all concerned with curriculum.

Clearly, an understanding of curriculum planning and curriculum development demands an understanding of the classroom (Westbury, 1979), but it is also necessary to place the determination of curriculum in a broader context. This includes local and national constraints, societal values and views on the appropriate selection of knowledge. The study of the curriculum cannot be undertaken without equal reference to both theory and practice.

BIBLIOGRAPHY

ADAMSON, J.W., *A Short History of Education*, Cambridge University Press, 1919.
ARIÈS, P., *Centuries of Childhood*, Jonathan Cape, 1962. (Penguin edition, 1973.)
ARNOLD, M., *Culture and Anarchy*, 1868-9, DOVER WILSON, J., ed., 1948 edition, Cambridge University Press.
ATKIN, J.M., 'Educational Accountability in the US', *Educational Analysis*, vol. 1, no. 1, Summer 1979.
AUSUBEL, D.P., *Educational Psychology A Cognitive View*, Holt, Rinehart and Winston, 1968.
BAGLEY, W.C., *Classroom Management*, Macmillan, New York, 1910.
BAMFORD, T.W., *Thomas Arnold on Education*, Cambridge University Press, 1970.
BANDURA, A., 'The Stormy Decade: Fact or Fiction', in MUSS, R.E., ed., *Adolescent Behaviour and Society*, 2nd edition, Random House, New York.
BANKS, O., *The Sociology of Education*, Batsford, 1963.
BANTOCK, G.H., *The Implications of Literacy*, Leicester University Press, 1965.
BARNES, D., *From Communication to Curriculum*, Penguin, 1976.
BARON, G., and HOWELL, D.A., *The Government and Management of Schools*, Athlone Press, 1974.
BARROW, R., 'Back to Basics', in BERNBAUM, G., ed., *Schooling in Decline*, Macmillan, 1979.
BELL, R., *Open University Course E283: Thinking About the Curriculum*, Open University, 1971.
BELL, R., and GRANT, N., *A Mythology of British Education*, Panther, 1974.
BERNSTEIN, B., 'Social class and linguistic development: a theory of social learning', in HALSEY, A.H., FLOUD, J., and ANDERSON, C.A., eds., *Education, Economy and Society*, Free Press of Glencoe, New York, 1961.
BERNSTEIN, B., 'A socio-linguistic approach to social learning', in GOULD, J. ed., *Penguin Survey of the Social Sciences*, Penguin, 1965.
BINET, A., and SIMON, T., *L'Année Psychologique*, vol. 2, 1905.

Bibliography

BLOCK, J.H., ed., *Mastery Learning*, Holt, Rinehart and Winston, 1971.
BLOOM, B.S., *et al.*, *Taxonomy of Educational Objectives*, Longman, 1956.
BLOOM, B.S., *Human Characteristics and School Learning*, McGraw-Hill, 1976.
BLOOM, B.S., HASTINGS, J.T., and MADAUS, G.F., *Handbook on Formative and Summative Evaluation of Student Learning*, McGraw-Hill, 1971.
BOBBITT, J.F., 'The elimination of waste in education', *Elementary School Journal*, 1912.
BOBBITT, J.F., *The Supervision of City Schools*. 12th Yearbook, NSSU, 1913.
BOBBITT, J.F., *The Curriculum*, Houghton Mifflin, 1918.
BOLAM, R., SMITH, G., and CANTER, H., 'Local Education Authority Advisers and Educational Innovation', *Educational Administration*, vol. 6, no. 1, Winter, 1977/8.
BOLAM, R., SMITH, G., and CANTER, H., *LEA Advisers and the Mechanics of Innovation*, National Foundation for Educational Research, 1978.
BRUNER, J.S., *The Process of Education*, Harvard University Press, Cambridge, Mass., 1961.
BRUNER, J.S., *Towards a Theory of Instruction*, Harvard University Press, Cambridge, Mass., 1966.
BRUNER, J.S., *Beyond the Information Given*, ANGLIN, J.M. ed., Allen and Unwin, 1974.
BRUNER, J.S., GOODNOW, J., and AUSTIN, S.A., *A Study of Thinking*, Wiley, 1956.
BRUNER, J.S., OLVER, R.R. and GREENFIELD, P.M., *Studies in Cognitive Growth*, Wiley, 1966.
BURT, C., *The Factors of the Mind*, University of London Press, 1940.
BURT, C., 'The Inheritance of Ability', *American Psychologist*, vol. 13, 1958.
BURT, C., *Mental and Scholastic Tests*, 4th edition, Staples Press, 1962.
CALLAHAN, R.E., *Education and the Cult of Efficiency*, University of Chicago Press, 1962.
CARROLL, J.B., 'A Model of School Learning', *Teachers College Record*, vol. 64, 1963.
CORBETT, A., *Whose Schools?*, Fabian Research Series, 328, 1976.
DALE, E., 'Historical setting of programmed instruction', in LARGE, P.C., ed., *Programmed Instruction, the 66th Yearbook of the National Society for the Study of Education*, Part II, University of Chicago Press, 1967.
DAVIES, I., 'Education and Social Science', *New Society*, 8 May 1968.
de MAUSE, L., *History of Childhood*, Psychohistory Press, USA, 1974. Souvenir Press edition, 1976.
DEPARTMENT OF EDUCATION AND SCIENCE, *Children and Their Primary*

Schools (Plowden Report), HMSO, 1967.
DEPARTMENT OF EDUCATION AND SCIENCE, *A New Partnership for our Schools* (Taylor Report), HMSO, 1977.
DEPARTMENT OF EDUCATION AND SCIENCE, *Curriculum 11-16,* HMSO, 1977.
DEPARTMENT OF EDUCATION AND SCIENCE, *Education in Schools. A Consultative Document,* HMSO, 1977.
DEPARTMENT OF EDUCATION AND SCIENCE, *School Examinations. Report of the Waddell Committee,* Vols. I and II, HMSO, 1978.
DEPARTMENT OF EDUCATION AND SCIENCE, *Local Authority Arrangements for the School Curriculum,* HMSO, 1979.
DEPARTMENT OF EDUCATION AND SCIENCE, *Primary Education in England,* HMSO, 1979.
DEPARTMENT OF EDUCATION AND SCIENCE, *Assessing the Performance of Pupils,* Report on Education No. 93, HMSO, 1978.
DEPARTMENT OF EDUCATION AND SCIENCE, *Aspects of Secondary Education in England,* HMSO, 1979.
DEPARTMENT OF EDUCATION AND SCIENCE, *A View of the Curriculum,* HMI Series: Matters for Discussion No. 11, HMSO, 1980.
DEPARTMENT OF EDUCATION AND SCIENCE, *A Framework for the School Curriculum,* DES, 1980.
DYSON, A.E., 'The Sleep of Reason', in COX, C.B., and DYSON, A.E., eds., *Fight for Education* (Black Paper 1), Critical Quarterly Society, 1969.
ELKIND, D., 'The development of quantitative thinking: a systematic replication of Piaget's studies', *Journal of Genetic Psychology,* vol. 98, 1961.
ELLIOTT, J., 'Preparing Teachers for Classroom Accountability', *Education for Teaching,* no. 100, Summer 1976.
ELLIOTT, J., 'Self-accounting Schools; are they possible?', *Educational Analysis,* vol. 1, no. 1, 1979.
ELLIOTT, J., 'Who should monitor performance in schools?', in SOCKETT, H., ed., *Accountability in the English Educational System,* Hodder and Stoughton, 1980.
ELLIS, A., 'Institutional Autonomy and Public Accountability — A Response', *Proceedings of the British Educational Administration Society,* Winter 1975.
ELLIS, T., HADDOW, B., McWHIRTER, J., and COLGAN, D., *William Tyndale: The Teachers' Story,* Writers and Readers Publishing Co-operative, 1976.
ENTWISTLE, H., *Child-Centred Education,* Methuen, 1970.
ERLENMEYER-KIMLING, L., and JARVIK, L.F., 'Genetics and intelligence: a review', *Science,* vol. 142, 1963.
EVETTS, J., *The Sociology of Educational Ideas,* Routledge and Kegan Paul, 1973.

Bibliography

EYSENCK, H.J., *The Structure of Human Personality*, Methuen, 1960.
FLAVELL, J.H., and WOHLWILL, J.S., 'Formal and functional aspects of cognitive development', in ELKIND, D., and FLAVELL, J.H., eds., *Studies in Cognitive Development*, Oxford University Press, 1969.
FORD, G.W., and PUGNO, L., *The Structure of Knowledge and the Curriculum*, Rand McNally, 1964.
FROEBEL, F., *The Education of Man*, 1826.
FLOUD, J.S., HALSEY, A.H., and MARTIN, F.M., *Social Class and Educational Opportunity*, Heinemann, 1957.
FRASER, E.D., *Home Environment and the School*, University of London Press, 1959.
GAGNÉ, R.M., *The Conditions of Learning*, 2nd edition, Holt, Rinehart and Winston, 1970.
GAGNÉ R.M., *Essentials of Learning for Instruction*, The Dryden Press, Holt, Rinehart and Winston, 1974.
GAGNÉ, R.M., and BRIGGS, L.J., *Principles of Instructional Design*, Holt, Rinehart and Winston, 1974.
GALTON, F., *Hereditary Genius*, Appleton, New York, 1870.
GATHORNE HARDY, J., *The Rise and Fall of the British Nanny*, Hodder and Stoughton, 1972.
GOLDSTEIN, H., and BLINKHORN, S., 'Monitoring educational standards: an inappropriate model', *Bulletin of the British Psychological Society*, vol. 30, 1977.
GOODLAD, J.I., *School, Curriculum, and the Individual*, Blaisdell Publishing Company, Mass., 1966.
GOODLAD, J.I., 'Introduction', in TAYLOR, P.H., and TYE, K.A., *Curriculum, School and Society*, National Foundation for Educational Research, 1975.
GORDON, P., and LAWTON, D., *Curriculum Change in the Nineteenth and Twentieth Centuries*, Hodder and Stoughton, 1978.
GRAY, H.L., *Change and Management in Schools*, Nafferton Books, Studies in Education, Driffield, Yorks., 1978.
GRETTON, J., and JACKSON, M., *William Tyndale: Collapse of a School or a System?*, Allen and Unwin, 1976.
GUILFORD, J.P., 'The structure of intellect', *Psychological Bulletin*, vol. 53, 1956.
HAMILTON, D., *et al, Beyond the Numbers Game*, Macmillan, 1977.
HARGREAVES, D.H., *Social Relations in a Secondary School*, Routledge and Kegan Paul, 1967.
HARRIS, K., *Education and Knowledge*, Routledge and Kegan Paul, 1979.
HEARNSHAW, L.S., *Cyril Burt: Psychologist*, Hodder and Stoughton, 1979.
HEBB, D.O., *The Organisation of Behaviour*, Wiley, New York, 1949.
HEIM, A.W., *The Appraisal of Intelligence*, Methuen, 1954.

HEIM, A.W., *Intelligence and Personality*, Penguin, 1970.
HIRST, P.H., 'Liberal Education and the Nature of Knowledge', in ARCHAMBAULT, R.D., ed., *Philosophical Analysis and Education*, Routledge and Kegan Paul, 1965.
HIRST, P.H., *Knowledge and the Curriculum*, Routledge and Kegan Paul, 1974.
HIRST, P.H., and PETERS, R.S., *The Logic of the Curriculum*, Routledge and Kegan Paul, 1970.
HOUSE, E.R., ed., *School Evaluation: The Politics and Process*, McCutchan, 1973.
HOUSE, E.R., *The Politics of Educational Innovation*, McCutchan, 1974.
HOUSE, E.R., 'Accountability in the USA', *Cambridge Journal of Education*, vol. 5, no. 2, Easter 1975.
HUMBLE, S., 'Governing Schools: Has the Taylor Report Got the Balance Right?', *Educational Administration*, vol. 6, no. 1, Winter 1977/8.
HUNT, J. McV., *Intelligence and Experience*, Ronald Press, New York, 1961.
INHELDER, B., and PIAGET, J., *The Growth of Logical Thinking*, Routledge and Kegan Paul, 1958.
INNER LONDON EDUCATION AUTHORITY, *William Tyndale Junior and Infant School Public Inquiry* (Auld Report), ILEA, 1976.
JACKSON, B., *Streaming: An Education System in Miniature*, Routledge and Kegan Paul, 1964.
JACKSON, B., and MARSDEN, D., *Education and the Working Class*, Routledge and Kegan Paul, 1962.
JENKINS, D., and SHIPMAN, M., *Curriculum: an introduction*, Open Books, 1976.
KING, R., *All Things Bright and Beautiful?*, John Wiley, 1978.
KOGAN, M., *The Politics of Educational Change*, Fontana, 1978.
LACEY, C., *Hightown Grammar: the school as social system*, Manchester University Press, 1970.
LASLETT, P., *The World We Have Lost*, 2nd edition, Methuen, 1971.
LASLETT, P., *Family Life and Illicit Love in Earlier Generations*, Cambridge University Press, 1977.
LAWRENCE, E., ed., *Friedrich Froebel and English Education*, University of London Press, 1952.
LAWTON, D., *Class, Culture and the Curriculum*, Routledge and Kegan Paul, 1975.
LAWTON, D., GORDON, P., ING, M., GIBBY, B., PRING, R., and MOORE, T., *Theory and Practice of Curriculum Studies*, Routledge and Kegan Paul, 1978.
LAWTON, D., *The Politics of the School Curriculum*, Routledge and Kegan Paul, 1980.

Bibliography

LESSINGER, L.M., 'Accountability for results', in LESSINGER, L.M., and TYLER, R.W., eds., *Accountability in Education*, Charles A. Jones, Washington, Ohio, 1972.

LOCKE, J., *Some Thoughts Concerning Education*, Cambridge University Press, 1880 edition.

LUNZER, E.A., 'Some points of Piagetian theory in the light of experimental criticism', *Child Psychology and Psychiatry*, vol. 1, 1960.

MACDONALD, B., 'Humanities Curriculum Project', in SCHOOLS COUNCIL, *Evaluation in Curriculum Development. Twelve Case Studies*, Macmillan, 1973.

MACINTOSH, H.G., and SMITH L.A., *Towards a Freer Curriculum*, University of London Press, 1974.

MACLURE, S., 'The Control of Education', in HISTORY OF EDUCATION SOCIETY, *Studies in the Government and Control of Education Since 1860*, Methuen, 1970.

MARSDEN, W.E., 'Education and Social Geography of Nineteenth Century Towns and Cities', in REEDER, D.A., ed., *Urban Education in the Nineteenth Century*, Taylor and Francis, 1977.

McCANN, P., ed., *Popular Education and Socialization in the Nineteenth Century*, Methuen, 1977.

MONTESSORI, M., *The Secret of Childhood*, Longmans Green, 1936.

MOORE, T.W., *Educational Theory: An Introduction*, Routledge and Kegan Paul, 1974.

MUSGROVE, F. *Youth and the Social Order*, Routledge and Kegan Paul, 1964.

NATIONAL UNION OF TEACHERS, *Partnership in Education*, National Union of Teachers, 1978.

NISBET, S., *Purpose in the Curriculum*, University of London Press, 1957, eighth impression, 1974.

NUNN, P., *Education: Its Data and First Principles*, Edward Arnold, 1920.

OPEN UNIVERSITY, Course E203 *Curriculum Design and Development*, Unit 28, 'Innovation and the Classroom...the Ford Teaching Project', Open University, 1976.

PARLETT, M., and HAMILTON, D., 'Evaluation as Illumination', in TAWNEY, D., ed., *Curriculum Evaluation Today: Trends and Implications*, Macmillan, 1976.

PATEMAN, T., ed., *Counter Course. A Handbook for Course Criticism*, Penguin, 1972.

PILE, W.D., *The Department of Education and Science*, Allen and Unwin, 1979.

PEAKER, G.F., 'The regression analyses of the national survey', in *Children and Their Primary Schools* (Plowden Report), Report of the Central Advisory Council for Education (England), HMSO, 1967.

PEEL, E.A., 'Experimental examination of some of Piaget's schemata concerning children's perception and thinking, and a discussion of their educational significance', *British Journal of Educational Psychology*, vol. 29, 1959.
PEEL, E.A., *The Pupil's Thinking*, 2nd edition, Oldbourne, 1968.
PEEL, E.A., *The Nature of Adolescent Judgment*, Staples, 1971.
PEEL, E.A., 'The Thinking and Education of the Adolescent', in VARMA, V.P., and WILLIAMS, P., eds., *Piaget, Psychology and Education*, Hodder and Stoughton, 1976.
PETERS, R.S., ed., *Perspectives on Plowden*, Routledge and Kegan Paul, 1968.
PIAGET, J., *Science of Education and the Psychology of the Child*, Longmans, 1971.
PIDGEON, D., and YATES, A., *An Introduction to Educational Measurement*, Routledge and Kegan Paul, 1968.
PINCHBECK, I., and HEWITT, M., *Children in English Society*, 2 vols., Routledge and Kegan Paul, 1969.
POPPER, K.R., *Conjectures and Refutations*, Routledge and Kegan Paul, 1963.
PRING, R., *Knowledge and Schooling*, Open Books, 1976.
RAND CORPORATION REPORT, *Federal Programs Supporting Educational Change*, vol. 8, US Government Printing Office, 1978.
REYNOLDS, J., and SKILBECK, M., *Culture and the Classroom*, Open Books, 1976.
RICHARDSON, E., *The Teacher, the School and the Task of Management*, Heinemann Educational, 1973.
RICHARDSON, E., *Authority and Organisation in the Secondary School*, Macmillan, 1975.
RICHMOND, W.K., *The School Curriculum*, Methuen, 1971.
ROSENTHAL, R., and JACOBSON, L., 'Teachers' expectancies: determinants of pupils' IQ gains', *Psychological Reports*, vol. 19, 1966.
ROUSSEAU, J.J., *Emile*, Everyman edition, 1911.
RUSK, R.R., *The Doctrines of the Great Educators*, Macmillan, 1969.
RUTHERFORD, W.L., 'Criterion-referenced programmes: the missing element', *Journal of Curriculum Studies*, vol. 11, no. 1, March 1979.
SCHOOLS COUNCIL, *Enquiry No. 1*, HMSO, 1968.
SCHOOLS COUNCIL, *Science 5-13 Curriculum Project: With Objectives in Mind*, Macdonald, 1972.
SCHOOLS COUNCIL, *Examinations at 16+: proposals for the future*, Schools Council, 1975.
SCHRAMM, W., *The Research on Programmed Instruction. An Annotated Bibliography*, US Government Printing Office, 1964.

Bibliography

SCHWAB, J.J., 'Structure of the Discipline. Meaning and Significance', in FORD, G.W., and PUGNO, L., *The Structure of Knowledge and the Curriculum*, Rand McNally, 1964.

SHAW, K., 'Managing the Curriculum in Contraction', in RICHARDS, C., ed., *Power and the Curriculum: Issues in Curriculum Studies*, Nafferton Books, 1978.

SHORTER, E., *The Making of the Modern Family*, Collins, 1976.

SIMON, B., 'The History of Education', in TIBBLE, J.W., ed., *The Study of Education*, Routledge and Kegan Paul, 1966.

SIMONS, H., 'School-Based Evaluation on Democratic Principles', *Curriculum Action Research Network*, Bulletin 2, Cambridge Institute of Education, 1978.

SKEMP, R.R., *Intelligence, Learning and Action*, Wiley, 1979.

SMITH, M., *The Underground and Education. A Guide to the Alternative Press*, Methuen, 1977.

SNEYD, G.A., *A Relation, or rather a true account of the Island of England*, Camden Society No. 37, 1847.

SOCKETT, H., 'Behavioural Objectives', *London Educational Review*, vol. 2, no. 3, Autumn 1973.

SOCKETT, H., ed., *Accountability in the English Educational System*, Hodder and Stoughton, 1980.

SPEARMAN, C., '"General intelligence" objectively determined and measured', *American Journal of Psychology*, vol. 115, 1904.

SPENCER, H., *Education: Intellectual, Moral and Physical*, 1861. Reprinted Williams and Norgate, 1889.

SPRINGHALL, J., *Youth, Empire and Society. British Youth Movements 1883-1940*, Croom Helm, 1977.

STENHOUSE, L., *An Introduction to Curriculum Research and Development*, Heinemann, 1975.

STENHOUSE, L., 'School Mastery', review in *The Times Educational Supplement*, 6 January 1978.

STONE, L., *The Crisis of the Aristocracy 1558-1641*, Oxford University Press, 1965.

TAPPER, E.R., *Young People and Society*, Faber and Faber, 1971.

TAWNEY, D., ed., *Curriculum Evaluation Today. Trends and Implications*, Macmillan, 1976.

TAYLOR, C., *The Explanation of Behaviour*, Routledge and Kegan Paul, 1964.

TAYLOR, P.H., and RICHARDS, C., *An Introduction to Curriculum Studies*, National Foundation for Educational Research, 1979.

THRING, E., *Life, Diary and Letters of Edward Thring*, PARKIN, G.R., ed., vol. 1, Macmillan, 1898.

TOMLINSON, J., *Education in Cheshire*, Summer 1979.

Bibliography

TYLER, R., *Basic Principles of Curriculum and Instruction*, University of Chicago Press, 1949.

van der EYKEN, W., *Education, the Child and Society. A Documentary History 1900-1973*, Penguin, 1973.

VARMA, V.P., and WILLIAMS, P., eds., *Piaget, Psychology and Education*, Hodder and Stoughton, 1976.

VERNON, P.E., *The Measurement of Abilities*, 2nd edition, University of London Press, 1956.

VERNON, P.E., *Secondary School Selection. A British Psychological Society Inquiry*, Methuen, 1957.

VERNON, P.E., 'Abilities and attainments in the Western Isles', *Scottish Educational Journal*, vol. 48, 1965.

VERNON, P.E., 'Educational and intellectual development among Canadian Indians and Eskimos', *Educational Review*, vol. 18, 1966.

VERNON, P.E., 'A cross-cultural study of "creativity tests" with 11 year old boys', *New Research in Education*, vol. 1, 1967.

WARBURTON, F.W., 'The ability of the Gurkha recruit', *British Journal of Psychology*, vol. 42, 1951.

WARNOCK, M., *Schools of Thought*, Faber, 1977.

WASON, P.C., 'Reasoning', in FOSS, B., ed., *New Horizons in Psychology*, Penguin, 1966.

WATSON, F., *The Old Grammar Schools*, Cambridge University Press, 1916. Reprinted, F. Cass, 1968.

WATSON, P., 'How race affects IQ', *New Society*, 16 July, 1970.

WESTBURY, I., 'Research into classroom processes: a review of ten years' work', *Journal of Curriculum Studies*, vol. 10, no. 4, December 1978.

WHITE, J.P., 'The end of the compulsory curriculum', in *The Curriculum* (Doris Lee Lectures), Studies in Education (New Series) 2, University of London Institute of Education, 1975.

WHITFIELD, R., *Disciplines of the Curriculum*, McGraw-Hill, 1971.

WILLIAMS, R., *The Long Revolution*, Penguin, 1965.

WISEMAN, S., *Education and Environment*, Manchester University Press, 1964.

YOUNG, M.F.D., ed., *Knowledge and Control: New Directions for the Sociology of Education*, Collier-Macmillan, 1971.

Index

Accountability
  background, 78-9
  bureaucratic, 88-9
  Cambridge Accountability Project, 91
  democratic, 89-90
  evaluation, 88
  financial aspect, 81
  future of, 159-60
  industrial model, 82
  reasons for, 81-9
  teacher, 85
  in UK, 82-3, 85-8
  in USA, 88-92
Acts of Parliament
  Education Act (1870), 65
  Education (Provision of Meals) Act (1906), 65
  Education Act (1944), 75, 79, 99
  Factory Acts (1813, 1833), 65, 68
Adelman, C. 155-6
Adolescence
  discovery of, 68
  judgment, 126-8
Althorp, Lord, 76
Ariès, P. 61
Arnold, Matthew, 36
Arnold, Thomas, 13
Assessment of Performance Unit, 9, 77, 91-2, 110-11, 160
Atkin J. M. 87
Auld, R. 101
Ausubel, D. P.
  cognitive growth in primary children, 117-18
  and at secondary stage, 121-3
  and motivation, 138-9
  discovery learning, 143

Bamford, T. W. 13
Bandura, A. 69
Bantock, G. H. 40
Barnes, D. 161
Baron, G. 100
Barrow, R. 8
Becher, A. R. 90
Behaviourism, 30
Bernstein, B. 28
Binet, A. 20-1
Black Papers, 14, 77

Block, J. H. 145
Bloom, B. S. 143-5, 149
Bobbitt, J. F. 86, 106, 148
Bolam, R. 97
Broudy, H. S. 43-4
Brougham, Lord, 75
Bruner, J.
  cognitive growth, 115-19
  discovery learning, 142-3
  spiral curriculum, 116-17
  theory of instruction, 130-2
Burt, C. 22-3, 24

Callahan, R. E. 85-6
Carroll, J. B. 144
Case studies in evaluation, 156-7
Chesterfield, Lord, 63
Child-centred education, 19, 93
Childhood
  and adolescence, 68
  and curriculum, 60-72
  and innate goodness, 15-19
  and natural evil, 12-14
  psychogenic view of, 70
Children under Five in Public Elementary Schools Committee/Report, 65
Cognitive development
  Ausubel's theories, 117-19
  Bruner's theories, 115-17
  limitation of theories, 123-4
  Piaget's theories, 113-15
Comenius, J. A. 35
Committee of the Privy Council on Education, 76
Commons, House of, Expenditure Committee/Report, 78
Concept acquisition, 124-6
Corbett, A. 77-8
Crichton-Browne, J. Dr. 65
Crowther Committee/Report, 49
Culture
  and curriculum, 39-40, 109-11
  and education, 36
  'high', 51
  and intelligence, 29-30
Curricular Differences for Boys and Girls Committee/Report, 69
Curriculum Study Group, 76

Curriculum
  and childhood, 60-72
  classical, 33-4, 37
  and cognitive development in the primary years, 113-19
  and cognitive development in the secondary years, 119-29
  common, 46-7
  control of, 74-7, 79
  core, 94
  and culture, 39-40
  decision-making in, 93-103, 161
  definitions of, 7-8, 74
  elementary, 37
  evaluation, 147-57
  and examining bodies, 98-9, 160-1
  history of, 49-59
  integrated, 39
  intelligence and, 20-31
  and knowledge, 42-3
  and local education authority advisers, 97-8
  objectives, 39, 83, 136
  planning models, 105-11
  planning by behavioural objectives, 83-4
  politics of, 74-9
  primary school, 116-18, 159
  process or input model, 108
  problems of historical research, 52-4
  scientific, 34-5
  secondary schools, 126-8
  situational analysis or cultural analysis model, 109-11
  sociology of, 11-12
  theory, 162

Darwin, C. 37
Davies, I. 51
de Mause, L. 70-2
Department of Education and Science
  relationship with local education authorities and schools, 158-9
  Aspects of Secondary Education in England (1979), 7, 10, 79
  Assessing the Performance of Pupils (1978), 160
  Curriculum Differences for Boys and Girls, Education Survey No. 21 (1975), 69
  Curriculum 11-16 (1977), 46, 79, 94-5, 110-11
  Education in Schools. A Consultative Document (1977), 78, 93-4, 159-60
  A Framework for the School Curriculum (1980), 8, 159
  Local Authority Arrangements for the School Curriculum (1979), 78, 159
  Primary Education in England (1978), 8
Dewey, J. 66, 86
Douglas, J. W. B. 29-30
Durkheim, E. 12-13
Dyson, A. E. 15

Eccles, Sir David, 76
Education
  academic study of, 66
  citizenship and, 55
  consumerism in, 75
  demographic and economic influences on, 68
  early views on, 60-4,
  efficiency in, 86-7
  girls, 62, 68-9
  and ideologies, 50-2
  Marxism and, 54, 74
  models in, 83-4
  play and, 66-7
  standards in, 81
  theory, 42
  two traditions in, 51
Eisner, E. W. 162
Elliott, J. 91, 155-6
Ellis, A. 96-7
Enquiry No. 1, 96
Entwistle, H. 33
Epistemology, 42
Eraut, M. 90
Evaluation
  and accountability, 88, 90-1
  briefing decision-makers model, 152-4
  case study model, 156-7
  classical experimental model, 148-51
  definitions of, 147-8
  illuminative or social anthropological model, 151-2
  styles of, 153-4
  teacher as researcher, 154-6
Evetts, J. 11
Examinations
  Certificate of Secondary Education (CSE), 98, 160
  Common examination at 16+, 99, 160
  General Certificate of Education (GCE), 76, 82, 160
  School Certificate, 76
Examining bodies, 98-9
Eysenck, H. J. 11

Fabian Society, 77
Fitch, J. G. 65
Ford Teaching Project, 155-6
Froebel, F. 12, 16-18, 66

Gagné, R. M.
  comparison with Bruner's approach to curriculum, 136
  theory of instruction, 132-4
Galton, F. 22
Goodlad, J. I. 7, 161
Gorst, J. 65
Governors and curriculum decisions, 99-102
'Great Debate', 78
Guilford, J. P. 25

Hall, G. S. 69
Hamilton, D. 151
Hamilton, J. 77
Handbook of Suggestions for Teachers (1905), 75
Hartlib, S. 35
Headmasters
  relationship with local education authorities, 99-101
Hebb, D. O. 22
Heim, A. 26
Her Majesty's Inspectors (HMI), 75, 78-9, 100, 110
Hewitt, M. 63
Hirst, P. H. 39, 148
Hobbes, Thomas, 12
House, E. R. 86, 88
Howell, D. A. 100
Humble, S. 103
Hunt, J. McV. 26

Ingleby, D. 30-1
Inhelder, B. 115-16
In-service training, 160-1
Intelligence
  and ability, 25-6
  and culture, 29-30
  definition of, 26
  nature of, 8-9, 22-4, 55
  social class and, 28-9
  theory of, 26
  tests, 21-3, unreliability of, 27-8

Jackson, B. 30
Jenkins, D. 7, 156

Kay-Shuttleworth, J. P. (formerly Kay), 65, 76
Keohane Committee/Report, 160
King, R. 19
Kliebard, H. M. 106
Knowledge
  and curriculum, 42-3, 47-8
  divisions of, 37-8
  forms of, 44-6
  organization of, 42-8
  selection of, 33-41
  sociology of, 39-40, 74
Kogan, M. 77

Language
  and learning, 117-18
  and social class, 28
Laslett, P. 71-2
Lawton, D. 8, 12, 29, 109, 162
Learning
  and curriculum, 113-37
  discovery, 142-3
  individualized, 140-1
  and language, 117-18
  mastery, 143-6
  programmed, 139-40

Local education authorities
  advisers, 97-8
  and control of curriculum, 79, 97-8
  and examinations, 82
Locke, J. 63

McCann, P. 54
McDonald, B. 88, 152-3
Macintosh, H. G. 98
Maclure, S. 50
'Man: A Course of Study' (MACOS), 135
Mastery learning, 143-6
Merritt, J. E. 107
Michigan State Accountability System, 87-8
Montessori, M. 67
Moore, T. W. 42
Mulcaster, R. 62
Musgrove, F. 55, 68

National Union of Teachers (NUT), 76, 103
Newcastle Committee/Report, 76
Newsom Committee/Report, 23-4
Norwood Committee/Report, 23
Nunn, P. 66-7

Objectives
  behavioural, 83-4, 90
  and mastery learning, 145-6
  model in curriculum, 106-7, 136-7
  taxonomy of, 149-50
Overpressure controversy, 65

Parents
  initiating curriculum change, 101-3
  and schooling, 75, 92, 96-7
Parlett, M. 151-2
Payment by results, *see* Revised Code, 1862
Peaker, G. F. 29
Peel, E. A. 113, 123-4
  and adolescent judgment, 126-8
Pestalozzi, J. H. 66
Peters, R. S. 19, 39
Phenix, P. H. 44-6
Piaget, J.
  child development, 19
  cognitive growth and curriculum planning, 113-15, 123-4
Pidgeon, D. 27
Pinchbeck, I. 63
PLAN system, 141-2
Plowden Committee/Report, 19, 28-9, 96
Popham, W. J. 162
Pring, R. 39
Programmed instruction, 139-40
'Progressive' methods, 77
Psychology
  learning theories, 130-7
  motivational theories, 138-46
  radical critiques of, 30-1
  reformist moves in, 24-8

Rasch model, 92, 111
Reports
   Children Under Five Years of Age in Public Elementary Schools (1905), 65
   Curriculum Differences for Boys and Girls (1923), 69
   Crowther (1959), 49
   House of Commons Expenditure Committee (1976), 78
   Keohane (1979), 160
   Newcastle (1861), 76
   Newsom (1963), 23-4
   Norwood (1943), 23
   Plowden (1967), 19, 28-9, 96
   Taylor (1977), 75, 101-2
   Waddell (1978), 160
Revised Code (1862), 76, 87, 105
Reynolds, J. 40, 109
Richardson, E. 161
richmond, W. K. 123
Roebuck, J. 75
Rousseau, J. J. 12, 15-16, 64
Ruskin Speech (1976), 78
Rutherford, W. L. 161

Schools
   comprehensive, 68
   hierarchichal nature, 161
   self-evaluation, 90-1
Schools Council for Curriculum and Examinations, 76-9, 96, 98
   Examinations at 16+: Proposals for the Future (1975), 99
   Impact and Take Up Project, 151
   Science 5-13 Project, 107
Schwab, J. J. 43
Secondary School Regulations, 76
Shaw, K. 95-6
Shipman, M. D. 7
Shorter, E. 64
Simon, B. 50
Simon, T. 20-1
Simons, H. 90
Skilbeck, M. 40, 109, 162
Skinner, B. F. 139-40
Smith, L. A. 98
Sockett, H. 9, 83, 85, 88, 108
Spearman, C. 21, 24

Spencer, H. 37-9
Spiral curriculum, 116-17
Stake, R. 151, 154
Stenhouse, L. 7-8, 83, 84, 108, 136, 150, 154, 162
Stone, L. 61-2
Subjects, status of, 49-50

Taba, H. 107
Tameside, Greater Manchester, 97
Tapper, E. R. 68
Taxonomy of objectives, 149-50
Taylor Committee/Report, 75, 101-2
Taylor, P. H. 162
Teachers
   and Academic Boards, 94, 161
   and control of curriculum, 75, 77
   and decision-making on curriculum, 101
   and examining, 99
   and in-service training, 160-1
   and pupils, 161-2
   as researchers, 154-6
Teachers' unions, 79
Theories of instruction, 130-7
Thring, E. 14
Tomlinson, J. 159
Triangulation, 155-6
Tropp, A. 76
Tyler, R. W. 82-3, 106-7, 148-9

Vernon, P. E. 27-8, 29

Waddell Committee/Report, 160
Wallace, J. G. 114
Warnock, M. 41
Watson, F. 33-4
Wesley, J. 63
Westbury, I. 162
Wheeler, D. K. 107
White, J. 53, 76
Whitfield, R. C. 44-6
William Tyndale Primary School, 75, 78, 92, 100
Williams, R. 36, 50, 109

Yates, A. 27
'Yellow Book', 78